THE PLAYS OF A

Classical World Series

Aristophanes and his Theatre of the Absurd, Paul Cartledge
Art and the Romans, Anne Haward
Athens and Sparta, S. Todd
Athens under the Tyrants, J. Smith
Athletics in the Ancient World, Zahra Newby
Attic Orators, Michael Edwards
Augustan Rome, Andrew Wallace-Hadrill
Cicero and the End of the Roman Republic, Thomas Wiedemann
Classical Archaeology in the Field, S.J. Hill, L. Bowkett and
    K. & D. Wardle
Classical Epic: Homer and Virgil, Richard Jenkyns
Democracy in Classical Athens, Christopher Carey
Early Greek Lawgivers, John Lewis
Environment and the Classical World, Patricia Jeskins
Greece and the Persians, John Sharwood Smith
Greek and Roman Historians, Timothy E. Duff
Greek and Roman Medicine, Helen King
Greek Architecture, R. Tomlinson
Greek Literature in the Roman Empire, Jason König
Greek Tragedy: An Introduction, Marion Baldock
Greek Vases, Elizabeth Moignard
Julio-Claudian Emperors, T. Wiedemann
Lucretius and the Didactic Epic, Monica Gale
Morals and Values in Ancient Greece, John Ferguson
Mycenaean World, K. & D. Wardle
Plato's Republic and the Greek Enlightenment, Hugh Lawson-Tancred
Plays of Aeschylus, A.F. Garvie
Plays of Euripides, James Morwood
Plays of Sophocles, A.F. Garvie
Political Life in the City of Rome, J.R. Patterson
Religion and the Greeks, Robert Garland
Religion and the Romans, Ken Dowden
Roman Architecture, Martin Thorpe
Roman Britain, S.J. Hill and S. Ireland
Roman Frontiers in Britain, David Breeze
Roman Satirists and Their Masks, Susanna Braund
Slavery in Classical Greece, N. Fisher
Women in Classical Athens, Sue Blundell

Classical World Series

THE PLAYS
OF
AESCHYLUS

A.F. Garvie

Bristol Classical Press

First published in 2010 by
Bristol Classical Press
an imprint of
Gerald Duckworth & Co. Ltd.
90-93 Cowcross Street, London EC1M 6BF
Tel: 020 7490 7300
Fax: 020 7490 0080
info@duckworth-publishers.co.uk
www.ducknet.co.uk

© 2010 by A.F. Garvie

A catalogue record for this book is available
from the British Library

ISBN 978 1 85399 707 5

Typeset by Ray Davies
Printed and bound in Great Britain by
CPI Antony Rowe, Chippenham and Eastbourne

Contents

Introduction

Aeschylus is the oldest of the three great Greek tragedians. Born probably in 525 or 524 BC, he lived through the end of tyranny at Athens and the restitution of democracy. He took part in the battle of Marathon in 490 BC and probably also in the battle of Salamis in 480 BC, the subject of his *Persians*. During his life he made at least two visits to Sicily, and died there at Gela in 456 or 455 BC. Those who wish may believe the late story that he was killed by a tortoise, which an eagle dropped on his bald head, mistaking it for a rock on which to crack the tortoise's shell.

His first tragedies were presented in 499 BC, and his first victory in the tragic competition was gained in 484 BC. In all he may have composed between eighty and ninety plays, of which only six have survived, plus a seventh which is probably not a genuine work of Aeschylus. Fragments of many of the lost plays have been preserved, but of others only the titles are known. The present book will deal with the six plays in the chronological order of their first production: *Persians* (472 BC), the earliest Greek tragedy that has come down to us, *Seven against Thebes* (467 BC), *Suppliants* (probably 463 BC), and the three plays of the *Oresteia* trilogy, *Agamemnon*, *Libation Bearers* and *Eumenides* (458 BC). All of these dates are certain, with the exception of *Suppliants*. It used to be regarded as a very early play, but in 1952 a scrap of papyrus was discovered in Egypt which showed that it cannot have been produced before 470 BC. The likeliest date is 463 BC. The book contains also an essay on *Prometheus Bound*, a play whose attribution to Aeschylus seems never to have been questioned in antiquity, but which is now regarded by probably most, though not all, scholars as not the work of Aeschylus (see pp. 61-2). One should remember that all the six plays were written within a period of only fourteen years, and thus they all belong to Aeschylus' ripe maturity. We know little about his earlier work, and it is therefore dangerous to make assumptions about the course of his development as a playwright.

In this book I have adopted the format of my *Plays of Sophocles* in the same series. There are few references to secondary literature, and references to line numbers of the plays are given only when they seem to be essential. The translations are my own, and are based largely on D.L. Page's 1972 Oxford Classical Text, and M.L. West's 1990 Teubner text (corrected edn 1998).

Persians

Persians is the earliest surviving Greek tragedy, but it is not an early play of Aeschylus, as he was already about fifty years of age when he composed it. His other surviving plays, like many, though probably not all, of his lost plays, belong to connected trilogies, in which all three tragedies which he presented on the same occasion were connected with one another in their subject-matter. *Persians* is unusual in that the tragedies which accompanied it, *Phineus* and *Glaucus*, must have dealt, in the conventional way, with stories from Greek mythology, whereas *Persians* has a subject drawn from recent history, the great victory of the Greeks over the Persians in the sea-battle of Salamis in 480 BC, only eight years before the production of Aeschylus' play. A few 'historical' tragedies of this kind are known to have been written in the fifth century, and two, with themes drawn from the Persian Wars, were produced by Aeschylus' older contemporary Phrynichus, none of whose plays have survived. *Persians* is the only example that we have of this kind of non-mythological tragedy. Ever since the nineteenth century scholars have debated whether it is proper to describe it as a tragedy at all. To many of an older generation it was simply a patriotic celebration, in which Aeschylus encouraged his audience to rejoice over the discomfited Persians, and to laugh at their barbarian ways. More recently some have discerned a political purpose: Aeschylus' aim was to support the statesman Themistocles at a difficult time in his career, by reminding the audience of how his fleet had saved Athens eight years earlier. For others again the play marks an important step in the process whereby the Athenians, living in a democratic city, learned to define themselves and their culture in contrast to the decadent, luxury-loving, but enslaved barbarians. The contrast is certainly implicit in the play, but whether Aeschylus wrote it with this intention is another matter. I will start from the premise that *Persians* is indeed a tragedy, and that, whatever the patriotic democratic audience may have expected when it entered the theatre, as the play progressed, thanks to Aeschylus' skill as a dramatist, it came more and more to identify with the Persians as their fellow-human beings in their suffering.

In one sense it is a simple kind of tragedy – that of a fall from great prosperity to ruin, the type of tragedy which Aristotle in his *Poetics* recognised as being particularly effective. When a rich and powerful person falls one notices it most strikingly. The Great King Xerxes and his mighty, wealthy empire must have seemed to Aeschylus to be the ideal subject for such a theme. Structurally the play will lead us from the prosperity to the ruin in a more or less straight line, but not without at least one surprise along the way. And, although we start with the prosperity, there is from the very beginning, in accordance with Aeschylus' usual practice, foreboding among the characters as to how the end is going to turn out. His audiences, which will normally be familiar at least with the commonest myths from which he chooses his subjects, will forebode along with the characters, and as they come to identify with them, may even irrationally hope that things will turn out differently this time. *Persians* is unique in that every single person in the audience knew from the beginning that the Persian expedition was heading for disaster. What no one knows at the start is that Aeschylus is going to invite us to sympathise with the enemy in its disaster.

Most scholars who recognise that this is a genuine tragedy believe that it is a simple tragedy also in another sense. Aeschylus, they say, presents the comfortable moral that *hybris* is always punished by the gods, and that suffering is always to be seen as divine punishment for *hybris*; those who do not commit it can be sure of success and prosperity – a doctrine that is neither tragic nor true. The term *hybris*, often misleadingly translated as 'pride' or 'arrogance', describes primarily the deliberate infliction of dishonour on someone else, whether human or divine, often with the aim of establishing one's own superiority. Only indirectly does it describe an attitude of mind, when it seems to its victim to be tantamount to an action directed against him. Modern scholars, obsessed with finding in *hybris* a central theme of Greek tragedy, have tried too hard to define exactly what it was that Xerxes did wrong, so that he incurred the punishment of the gods. The word occurs only twice late on in the play, in a single speech from the Ghost of Xerxes' father Darius. Until, and after, the ghost-scene, all the emphasis is on the amoral view that suffering is bound to befall those who become too prosperous.

The play begins with the *parodos*, the entrance-song of the Chorus of elders, delivered for the first 64 lines in recitative anapaests as it marches into the *orchestra*, and from 65-139 sung in fully lyric metres. The central theme of the first section, which provides the framework of the second section, reflects the Chorus' pride in the splendour, wealth and antiquity of the Persian empire, while a long catalogue of warriors conveys a sense of the irresistible size and might of its army. But the framework of the first section, which turns into the central theme of the lyric section, already introduces foreboding. In line 1 we hear of the army that has 'gone to Greece'. The verb *oichomai* is often used to mean 'to be lost' or 'destroyed'. It will recur ominously at lines 13 and 60. The Chorus is worried because no word has been received from the army in Greece, and at the end of the first section, and as a kind of coda at the end of the whole composition, it presents a picture of Persian wives yearning for their husbands, and mourning them as if they were already dead – which, as the audience knows, they are. Xerxes set out to impose a yoke of slavery on Greece (50), and to transport his army he yoked the Hellespont with a marvellous bridge of boats. The yoke-metaphor will become a key image in the play. As a result a wife has become 'yoked all alone' (139), a splendid oxymoron, and later we shall learn that Xerxes has succeeded only in breaking the yoke of his chariot in Atossa's dream (196) and of his empire at 594. Above all, the Chorus explains in the centre of the lyric section that it fears the treacherous deceit of a god, leading Persia into a hunting-net from which there is no escape. Many scholars, in their attempt to find Xerxes' *hybris* as early as possible in the play, deduce that the Persians' destiny was to win wars only by land, so that the gods were offended by Xerxes' naval expedition. If this is correct, it is the only reference in the first part of the play to any fault committed by Xerxes. It was shown, however, in the nineteenth century that the crucial stanza is out of place in the manuscripts. The Chorus says rather that it was the divinely appointed destiny for them to win wars by both land and sea, and that it is their very success in doing so that worries them.

The *parodos* ends, and the Chorus-leader invites his fellows to sit down in or at 'this ancient building' to consider how the expedition is faring. The reference is evidently to a council-chamber, and it is hotly debated as to whether it is represented by a stage-building (*skene*) at the back of the *orchestra*, or whether we are simply to imagine it (according to one view we are to suppose that we are actually inside the building). A *skene* and its door are certainly not employed in the play, but that need not mean that they were not available for other playwrights to use if they so wished. It is difficult to see why it should be mentioned at all if it is not there. As the Chorus moves towards it, its intention is frustrated by the appearance of Atossa, the queen-mother, and we shall see that this is only the first of several frustrated intentions in the play. Atossa too is worried, and the foreboding builds up as she recounts her sinister dream, in which Xerxes tried to yoke two women to his chariot, one in Persian and the other in Greek dress. The latter resisted and broke the yoke, so that Xerxes fell out of the chariot. The symbolism is obvious. That Xerxes tore his clothes, while his dead father Darius stood beside him pitying him, will become significant later in the play. The dream is followed by an equally worrying omen in which Atossa saw an eagle, the bird of Zeus and the emblem of the Persian kings, being forced to take refuge at the altar of Apollo from a hawk, a bird associated with that most Greek of gods, Apollo. The Chorus-leader prepares the development of the plot by advising her to pray and make offerings to the Olympian gods and to the gods of the underworld. With splendid wishful thinking he judges that everything will turn out well. The scene ends with questions from Atossa about distant Athens. When the Chorus-leader tells her that the Athenians are called the subjects and slaves of no master, in other words that they have a demo-cratic constitution, she is at first reassured; how could an army without a master stand up against the discipline of the Persian host? But the reassurance soon turns to further anxiety when the Chorus-leader points out that such an army has already defeated the Persians at Marathon. At this point the Messenger arrives to turn the foreboding into horrible reality.

His summary statement that Persian prosperity along with the whole army has been destroyed introduces what will be a key word of the whole scene: 'it is firstly a *bad* thing to bring *bad* news'. The word *kakos* is not surprisingly no stranger to tragedy, but it occurs far more often in *Persians* than in any other play of Aeschylus. This summary statement also deter-mines the course of the central part of the play; first in a semi-lyric (*epirrhematic*) exchange the Chorus will briefly lament in lyric verse, while the Messenger in spoken dialogue metre will add his brief com-ments on the defeat. It is clear that we can expect a much fuller account to follow, and that this will lead to a full-scale ode of lamentation (see p. 14). In this double tragedy of Persia and Xerxes Aeschylus regularly deals with the two in that order. That is why the Chorus, as representative of Persia, is the first to respond to the Messenger, while Atossa remains silent, and why, when she does intervene, her first thoughts are for her son Xerxes, whom she will represent until his own appearance at the end of the play. Despite some scholars, the arrangement has nothing to do with Aeschylus' supposed incompetence in the handling of his second actor.

The Messenger's four long speeches form the centrepiece of the whole play. For most of the time he speaks as the conventional tragic messenger. To remind us that he is addressing a stage- as well as a theatre-audience the speeches are separated by brief dialogues between the Messenger and Atossa. In these, the first attempts are made to apportion responsibility for the disaster: some nameless god must have been responsible. In his longest speech the Messenger specifically cites the resentment (*phthonos*) of the gods as the cause.

Occasionally the Messenger reminds us that he was an eyewitness of the events which he describes. This is in fact the only surviving tragedy in which the playwright was himself an eyewitness of the events which his stage-messenger reports. Historians have not surprisingly been concerned to evaluate Aeschylus' account in comparison with that of the later historian Herodotus, especially when there are differences between them. Probably neither is to be trusted uncritically. Aeschylus writes as a poet, not a historian, and it is his poetic purpose that determines the Messenger's reports.

In the first of his long speeches the Messenger presents a list of casualties, a catalogue that balances the list of names in the anapaestic section of the *parodos*. Now we know that those who went out in pride and confidence to war will not return. Aeschylus presents them not as cowardly barbarians, but as brave men who did not deserve their fate.

The second, the longest and most important, of his speeches describes the sea-battle. He begins with the secret message sent by Themistocles to Xerxes the day before the battle to entice him to fight in the narrows, and moves swiftly to describe sunset on the eve of battle. We end with the next sunset, which brings the battle to a close. In between the Messenger presents an elaborate picture of the sunrise that marked its beginning, the sunrise that was meant to bring victory to the Persians, but instead revealed the advancing confident Greeks. The symbolism of light and darkness is clear. Light belongs to the Greeks, and the darkness of disaster and defeat to the Persians. And throughout all this we are made to hear the sounds of the battle, the splashing of the oars, the confident paean of the Greeks, the great patriotic cry of 402-5, the confused babble of the Persian host, and finally the cries of lamentation, to which only the darkness of night could put a stop.

In his third speech the Messenger narrates the destruction of the contingent of Persians landed on the small island of Psyttaleia to despatch any shipwrecked Greeks who might struggle ashore. In Herodotus this appears as only a minor sideshow in the battle. It has therefore seemed surprising that Aeschylus prefaces his account by saying that what happened there was twice as bad as the sea-battle itself. Some have thought that his aim was to compliment the statesman Aristeides, who, according to Herodotus, led the force (specifically of hoplites) which annihilated the Persians. But Aeschylus says nothing about Aristeides, and it is much more likely that he makes so much of the incident because as a land-battle he wanted it to balance the sea-battle. In the *parodos* it was the Persians' destiny to win wars by land as well as by sea; now they have been defeated by land and sea. Moreover, on Psyttaleia it was not just the allies, as in the sea-battle, who were killed, but the cream of Persian nobility. The Messenger reports that Xerxes, who had watched the whole affair, tore his clothes. Atossa's dream has come true.

The final speech describes the horrendous journey endured by Xerxes and the remnant of the Persians back to the Hellespont. Almost certainly Aeschylus exaggerates the suffering. In particular the drowning of so many men as they attempted to cross the frozen river Strymon is probably his own invention. That the river froze over at that latitude in early November is very unlikely. According to Aeschylus the sun came up and melted the ice as the army was crossing. As at Salamis it is the sun that spells disaster for the Persians. Later in the play we shall learn that a large number of Persians were left behind in Greece under Mardonius. Aeschylus says nothing about them here. The impression that he wishes to give is that of almost total disaster, with only a tiny remnant managing to escape to Asia.

In the speech which ends the episode, Atossa rebukes the Chorus for its wishful thinking earlier in the play, and for its futile advice to make offerings to the gods. Nevertheless, although what is done cannot be undone, she will still make the offerings in the hope that things may turn out better in future. The audience shudders; for it knows that what the future holds in store for the Persians is the further defeat at Plataea. Atossa's wishful thinking is as futile as that of the Chorus. She leaves the stage to fetch the offerings from the palace, instructing the Chorus that, if Xerxes should arrive before her return, it should escort the king safely home. It will come as a surprise to the audience, as it does to modern scholars, that the instruction turns out to be unnecessary. We are to be kept waiting for Xerxes' arrival. The fulfilment of the initial foreboding may seem to be complete as far as Persia is concerned, but this is the tragedy also of Xerxes, and that has still to be developed. We look forward to his arrival, which will form the climax of the play.

The Chorus, in its full-scale ode of lamentation, blames Xerxes for the disaster, and for the first time contrasts him, as the failure, with his glorious and successful father. Aeschylus is preparing us for the ghost-scene that will follow. By dramatic convention the audience must forget that the real Darius was by no means as successful as the Chorus suggests. In particular the Chorus raises the question that will never receive a proper answer: why was Darius a success, when Xerxes failed? Atossa returns to the stage with her offerings, and for the first time we learn that they are to be used to call up Darius' Ghost from the underworld. The audience's attention is now focused on his tomb, which must have been present, probably as a temporary construction in the *orchestra*, from the beginning of the play. While Atossa makes the offerings, the Chorus summons him in a necromantic ritual which may suggest to the audience an oriental practice, but which was also traditional in Greece. In such rituals the difficulty of persuading the dead to hear is often stressed, and flattery is used to attract their attention. But Aeschylus has not simply incorporated a religious ritual into his text; he has adapted it to his dramatic purpose, as the Chorus' flattery of Darius helps to establish the contrast between Darius and his miserable son. The appearance of the Ghost, with his royal tiara and his saffron slippers, is one of the highlights of the play.

As always, the Chorus, representing Persia, is the first to respond to Darius' questions. But, when it is too awed to answer them, Atossa takes over for the rest of the scene, which will be concerned with Xerxes in particular. The Ghost has three functions to perform. First, by the very splendour of his presence he marks the contrast with his son, who will shortly appear in his rags, the son who, as we hear from Darius, is inferior not only to his father but to all the previous Persian kings. Secondly, he will predict the forthcoming disaster, when the Persians left behind in Greece, about whom we hear now for the first time, will be utterly destroyed at Plataea. The foreboding, which we may have thought had come to fulfilment with the news of Salamis, is now renewed, and will indeed continue beyond the end of the play.

Thirdly, the Ghost will provide a moral interpretation of the tragedy. In building the bridge over the Hellespont Xerxes offended Poseidon the god of the sea, and in destroying the temples of the gods at Athens the Persians committed *hybris*. Still in the context of *hybris* he goes on to say that to despise one's present fortune and to seek for more is bound to lead to the loss even of what one has. Moralists in the audience, like many modern scholars, may have seen in this *the* moral of the play. In retrospect, they can say that since Xerxes has brought ruin on his country, and since such ruin is always the result of bad behaviour, he must have done something morally wrong, whether we decide that it was the building of the bridge, or his crossing of the sea, or the attempt to enslave Europe as well as Asia, or, more probably, the enterprise as a whole. We should, however, be cautious in supposing that the play really has so simple a 'moral'. The whole of the first part of the play presented an alternative explanation, that it is not bad behaviour but success itself that is danger-ous. Neither idea is of much practical use as we try to ensure success and happiness in our own lives. It is only after Xerxes falls that we can decide that he must have crossed the line separating prosperity from excessive prosperity, and so incurred the resentment of the gods; or, for moralists like Darius, that he must have done something wrong to incur their punishment. But Darius' moral will be slightly undercut in the ode that follows his departure, as the Chorus sings of happier days when Darius invaded Europe, and sent his troops across the sea to conquer the Aegean islands. If it was wrong for Xerxes to do this, why was it acceptable for his father? After the departure of the Ghost no more will be heard of the 'moral'. Before he goes, he instructs Atossa to return to the palace to fetch a change of clothes for Xerxes, who is now in rags. She agrees to do so, saying that this is the worst thing that she has heard. So, at the end of one scene, Aeschylus prepares us for the next.

Before Xerxes enters, the Chorus sings the ode which takes us back to the glorious reign of Darius. If the play as a whole is built on the contrast between initial prosperity and final ruin, Aeschylus drives home that contrast by juxtaposing the two at the end. Xerxes enters, on foot, almost certainly alone, and in the rags that are the symbol of his utter failure. Fresh clothing might have been a symbol of rehabilitation but Atossa has failed to meet him. Not for the first time, but here most strikingly, an intention has been frustrated. It is to this moment that all the references to clothes throughout the play have been leading. In a remarkable example of an antiphonal *kommos*, a ritual lyric dirge shared between an actor and a chorus, Xerxes and the elders confront each other. The Chorus blames him for the deaths of so many men, who are listed in the third, and fullest, catalogue of names. But this ritual form too is adapted by Aeschylus to his dramatic purpose, as the tragedy of Persia and the tragedy of Xerxes finally come together. The music and the choreography are lost to us, but it is clear even from the rhythms and the language that the whole composition must have been highly effective on the stage. The tempo gradually increases, until each stanza is divided into lyric stichomythia, with each party singing single lines in rapid counterpoint. The rhythms become more broken and, as the *kommos*, and the play, come to an end, articulate language breaks down altogether. Then, as the whole company disappears from the *orchestra*, there is a final silence, which may remind us of the silence that ended the Messenger's report of the sea-battle. Some scholars have found a sense of closure, and hope for the future, in the coming together of King and Chorus. Rather, they come together only in their mourning. And, as the audience knows, it is Plataea that lies ahead.

Seven against Thebes

Seven against Thebes was the third member of a trilogy of connected tragedies, the first two being *Laius* and *Oedipus*. The satyr-play which followed the trilogy was the *Sphinx*, the monster killed by Oedipus, who consequently became king of Thebes and married his mother Jocasta, having previously unwittingly killed his father Laius. In the myth, after Oedipus' death his sons, Eteocles and Polyneices, inherited the throne. They quarrelled, and Polyneices went off to Argos, whence, having married the daughter of king Adrastus, he returned to Thebes with an Argive army, commanded by the 'Seven against Thebes'; and the two brothers killed each other in single combat at the seventh gate. The story was the subject of lost epic poems, and there are allusions to it earlier in Homer's *Odyssey*.

Little is known about Aeschylus' treatment of the events in the two earlier plays. *Laius* almost certainly dealt with Oedipus' killing of his father Laius, who had three times been warned by Apollo's Delphic Oracle that if he died without issue he would save, or keep safe, his city (see *Seven* 742-91). In his folly Laius ignored the warning, and Oedipus was born. We cannot tell whether, as in a version of the story that first appears in Euripides, a curse laid on Laius by Pelops preceded the consultations with the oracle. *Oedipus* must have dealt, as in Sophocles, with Oedipus' discovery of the fact that the man whom he had killed was his father, and that his wife was also his mother. In Aeschylus he continued to live on in Thebes after he had blinded himself. When he became angry with his sons, Polyneices and Eteocles, apparently over the way that they were treating him (786; the meaning, however, is disputed), he cursed them both, perhaps in the form of a riddle: they would divide the property with iron, which turns out in our play to be the sword, the Scythian stranger of 727-8 (cf. 941-6).

In the surviving play Aeschylus shows no interest in the rights and wrongs of the quarrel between Eteocles and Polyneices. Both brothers claim to have justice on their side, and when Amphiaraus condemns Polyneices (see p. 22) it is only for bringing a foreign army against his motherland. Eteocles appears as the legitimate ruler of Thebes. But they are united in their deaths, and in the final scene the Chorus mourns them both. We shall not see the brothers confront each other on stage. The only on-stage conflict that is presented is that between Eteocles and the Chorus of his supporters.

The original audience, which had seen the first two plays, was better informed than we are as to what to expect as *Seven* begins, particularly as it concerns the Curse of Oedipus. Aeschylus, however, probably surprises it. In the whole of the first part of the play the Curse will be almost totally forgotten, so that when our attention is at last turned to it, it will come as a shock. The play, unlike *Persians*, opens with a prologue in iambic dialogue metre, the first half of which comprises a speech from Eteocles, the protagonist, addressing the people of Thebes. Probably these are represented by a few on-stage extras, less probably by an off-stage audience, and less probably still by the theatre audience, which could hardly be sent off by Eteocles to take up position on the ramparts at 38 or 77. The theatre audience learns that the speaker is Eteocles (he names himself at 6), that Polyneices and his army are at the gates, and that the prophet Teiresias predicts an imminent enemy attack. So the present situation is revealed. More important, we learn that Eteocles is a good king, the responsible captain of the ship of state, the metaphor which begins, and will recur throughout, the play. He understands that when things go well the gods are held to be responsible, but if things turn out badly he himself will be blamed.

The second half of the prologue begins with a report from a Scout that the attack is indeed imminent. The seven Argive champions were drawing lots (a motif that will recur throughout the play) to decide which was to lead the attack at each of the seven city-gates. The plot has already begun to move. Eteocles, says the Scout, must be the wise helmsman of the ship. Clearly the city looks to him for its salvation. There is no real dialogue between the two men. We are not interested in the relationship between them. Instead, Eteocles' brief response takes the form of a prayer to various gods not to allow the city to be destroyed and to go under the yoke of slavery (a metaphor familiar from *Persians*). It is in the gods' interest to save Thebes; for a prosperous city honours the gods (a *quid pro quo* argument that will recur in the play). The prologue thus ends with the attention of both Eteocles and the audience concentrated on the fate of the city. We cannot, however, entirely ignore the fact that one of the deities to whom Eteocles prays is the Curse, the mighty Erinys (avenging goddess of his father). This will be the only reference to it for several hundred lines. Some find significance in the little word *ge*, 'at least'; 'at least do not destroy the city', says Eteocles. Does that imply 'whatever you may do with me'? But this may be too subtle a point for an audience to take in. Anyway, with the single reference to the Erinys, the second part of the play is already being prepared. What matters now is that Eteocles puts his city first.

After the presentation of the calm and manly resolution of Eteocles the *parodos* (entrance song of the Chorus) introduces a dramatic change of mood. The Chorus of panic-stricken and uncontrolled young women rushes into the *orchestra*, to present us with a highly emotional and vivid picture of war as seen from the point of view of the besieged inhabitants, much of it in the most excited of all Greek lyric metres, the dochmiac. It describes for us the dust raised by the advancing enemy, and the chaotic noise made by their weapons and the horses' bridles and the creaking of the chariot-axles. We should not ask how the Chorus can have seen and heard all this from its position inside the city. There is no way in which a Greek tragedian can present war visually to an audience, and there is nothing in Greek tragedy like the battle-scenes of Shakespeare. But the Chorus more than compensates with its purely verbal description, and presumably with its choreography. In its panic it has nothing to say about the king, or about the Curse. Its only recourse is to pray to the various deities whose statues are evidently displayed in the *orchestra*, perhaps on some kind of raised mound. The description and the prayers are interwoven throughout the composition. The Chorus' prayers are very different from the dignified prayer of Eteocles with which the prologue ended. Throughout the first part of the play, this will be the function of the Chorus, to provide a foil or background for the behaviour of Eteocles. The city needs him, but he is an isolated figure, and it is clear that his first task will be to restore discipline and morale in the citizen-body.

This sets the theme of the first episode. Eteocles angrily rebukes the Chorus for setting a bad example to the citizens, and for endangering the city by lowering morale. The Chorus continues to describe the sounds and sights, and to insist on the necessity of appealing to the gods. It has sometimes been thought that Eteocles' attitude to the gods comes close to dangerous blasphemy. The original audience may well have felt that he goes too far in his statement that to sacrifice to the gods is a matter for men, not women (230-1). A modern audience or reader may feel that he reveals an unattractive misogyny throughout the scene, and some have thought that the ancient audience might suspect that it was connected with Eteocles' own incestuous origins. But his view that women should keep silent and stay at home would not seem so strange in 467 BC. Pericles says something very similar in his Funeral Oration in Thucydides Book 2. We should certainly not look here for the reason for his fall, as if the gods were rightly punishing him for his behaviour. Eteocles, as the responsible ruler, has no choice but to suppress the indiscipline and ill-omened cries that are threatening the city, and to insist that it is his duty, that it cannot be left to the gods, to take the required action. So the male, virile Eteocles is contrasted with the weak, female Chorus. The Chorus' prayer for the city will in fact be heard, but it does not pray for Eteocles, who will be destroyed.

Throughout all this the plot does not develop at all, but it is by no means monotonous. Aeschylus constantly varies the pace. There are three ways in which an actor in Greek tragedy can interact with a chorus, and Aeschylus here employs all three. First, Eteocles responds to the Chorus' *parodos* with a long speech that sets the tone for what follows. Secondly, they engage more closely with each other in an *epirrhematikon*, in which the Chorus sings excitedly, while Eteocles speaks, as befits his role, in the iambic metre of normal dialogue. Thirdly, they come closer together in line-by-line stichomythia. In later tragedy this technique is often used for rapid, excited dialogue, but here the tone is calmer than in the *epirrhematikon*, and it thus leads on to a final speech from Eteocles, in which some kind of understanding is reached.

At the very end of this scene Aeschylus, as he often does, prepares us for the development that will occur in the next episode. Eteocles says, in ambiguous language, either that he is going off to arrange off stage for the appointment of six Theban champions to match the Argive champions, with himself as seventh, or that when he returns from wherever he is going he will make the arrangements on stage. The significance of the ambiguity will become apparent only later. The audience, which knows that the seventh gate was traditionally where the brothers killed each other, may shudder at the words 'and myself as seventh', but even here Eteocles' intention is not entirely clear; the Greek phrase could mean simply 'seven men including myself'. Either way, the audience will prepare itself for the appointment of the champions to lead to the fatal encounter between the two brothers at the seventh gate. We are, however, kept waiting while the Chorus, left alone in the *orchestra*, sings an ode in obedience to Eteocles' instructions in his final speech that it should calmly sing a holy paean, a confident prayer, to the gods. The tone in fact turns out to be almost as emotional as in the *parodos*, and again the Chorus presents us with a verbal description of the horrors of war, this time looking to the future as it visualises the terrible things that happen to the inhabitants of a city captured by an enemy.

At 369 Eteocles and the Scout return simultaneously but from opposite sides of the *orchestra*, each introduced by a different semi-chorus. So begins the remarkable second episode, about 300 lines long, which will take us from the first part of the play, in which all the emphasis is on the city, to the second part, which is almost totally concerned with the Curse and the fate of Eteocles. It consists of seven pairs of highly symmetrical speeches, of roughly the same length, in each of which a speech from the Scout describing one of the Argive champions, and the emblems on his shield, is followed by a response from Eteocles, in which he announces the appointment of an appropriate Theban champion to meet him. Between each pair of speeches the Chorus comments in lyric metre. Scholars are divided as to what is actually happening on stage. Are we to suppose that Eteocles is merely announcing arrangements that he has already made in his absence during the Chorus' song, or is it only now, in front of the audience, that he reaches his decisions? And has he brought with him the six other champions, to be sent off one by one to their respective posts? This last is improbable; Eteocles must be shown as an isolated figure. But on the answer to the first question depends our interpretation of the responsibility of Eteocles himself for his tragedy. If the arrangements have already been made while Eteocles was off stage, before he learned which Argive was at which gate, the remarkable appropriateness of the choice of each Theban defender must seem to be a matter of happy chance (at 508 he credits Hermes, the god of luck, with bringing the right Theban to serve at the fourth gate), or, as the audience must surmise, of fate; the Curse is working through what only *appears* to be the decisions of Eteocles. But if, on the other hand, Eteocles is making his decisions only now, and carefully matching each defender to the Scout's description of his opponent, it is reasonable to argue that he has nobody but himself to blame when he finds himself matched with Polyneices. It seems impossible to solve the problem. That the decision was made off stage is indicated by the past tenses at 448, 473, 505, and 508, and that it is being made on stage by the future or quasi-future tenses at 395, 408, 435-6, 472, and 621. It is not very satisfactory to suppose that some but not all of the appointments have already been made, or that he has already made his decisions in his mind but not yet acted upon them, or that he has chosen six champions but not yet assigned them to specific gates. The likeliest view is that Aeschylus deliberately leaves the matter unclear. By suggesting both that Eteocles is fated to fulfil the Curse, and that he is himself responsible for what happens to him, Aeschylus indicates that the responsibility is doubly determined. For this important aspect of his tragic thinking, see p. 70. Part of Eteocles' tragedy is that it is in trying to do his duty as a responsible ruler that he brings about the fulfilment of the Curse.

He takes care to choose in every case the appropriate defender, but the appropriateness has already been determined.

At the beginning of the episode the audience perhaps expects a rapid transition to the theme of the Curse. But its very length ensures that we almost forget what we know is going to happen. Most of our attention is devoted to the skilful way in which Eteocles is able to turn to his own advantage the powerful symbolism of the emblems on his hybristic enemies' shields, so that they come to symbolise not victory but defeat and death. The night, for example, on Tydeus' shield becomes the night that will fall upon his eyes when he dies. When (397) Eteocles begins his response with 'I would not dread any man's splendid array', the first person 'I' may give us momentary hope that he means to confront Tydeus himself. When we come to Eteoclus, the third Argive champion, we might again begin to hope that the Curse can be averted altogether. To the Greeks a person's name was believed to reveal something about its bearer's character or fate. In no known earlier version of the Seven against Thebes does Eteoclus occur, and he is never firmly established as one of the Seven. Even if Aeschylus did not actually invent him, his inclusion here must surely mislead the audience; what person could be more appropriate to confront him than the almost identically named Eteocles. But the moment passes. After the fifth pair of combatants has been dealt with we realise that there are only two to go. If Eteocles is to have any hope now, he must appoint himself to meet the sixth. But the sixth turns out to be Amphiaraus, who does not lend himself to the scornful demolition that Eteocles has practised on the first five. He is a good man, and a reluctant participant in the expedition. In the myth he is not killed, but disappears mysteriously into the ground. Eteocles can only deplore the company that he keeps. The note of confidence has changed to one of sadness. It is in the Scout's sixth speech (at 574) that the word *Erinys* occurs for the first time since 70, and that Polyneices is named for the first time in the play, when Amphiaraus points out (577-9) the significance of his name, 'the man of much strife'. There can be no question of Eteocles confronting Amphiaraus. We come, then, to the seventh pair of speeches, in which Aeschylus confirms what we really knew all along, that the only appropriate opponent for Polyneices is his brother Eteocles. In his last words (652) the Messenger reminds Eteocles, and the audience, of his duty to be captain of the ship of state.

The emotional outburst of Eteocles at 652-5, as he recognises the fulfilment of his father's Curse, marks the great climax of the play. It does not even occur to him that he might survive the duel. But then he immediately regains control of himself, and returns to his role as the responsible commander-in-chief, as he proceeds to give rational grounds for this his final appointment: justice is on his side, not that of Polyneices. He calls for his greaves to be brought. Many believe that he puts on all his armour during the following *epirrhematikon*, but this would distract us from Eteocles' dispute with the Chorus. Nor can he have arrived on stage already wearing his armour except for the greaves; for in epic poetry and in art the greaves are always the first to be put on. To the Chorus his decision seems to be madness. In the brief *epirrhematikon*, and an even shorter stichomythia, it tries to dissuade him from confronting his brother. The *epirrhematikon* balances the earlier one (see p. 20), and the Chorus, more excited than Eteocles, sings again in the same emotional dochmiac metre. But in this second confrontation between Eteocles and the Chorus the roles are reversed. In the earlier one Eteocles tried, with some success, to persuade the frightened young women to control themselves. Now it is the Chorus' turn to try to persuade Eteocles to abandon his mad plan, and it will be totally unsuccessful in its attempt. Some scholars have objected to this apparent change of choral personality. Here it behaves more like the conventional tragic chorus. In addressing Eteocles as 'my son' at 686, it seems to have forgotten that it is supposed to consist of young women. But the character of the Chorus is of no interest to the audience; it changes now because the situation has changed. Its role is still to provide a foil for him, and a background for his behaviour. The Chorus cannot understand why Eteocles cannot appoint someone else to face Polyneices. As for the Erinys, perhaps the gods may be persuaded by sacrifices to send her elsewhere. But Eteocles is adamant. Aeschylus presents no inner conflict. It has sometimes been held that we see him consciously taking upon himself the guilt of fulfilling the Curse and sacrificing himself in order to save his city, but there is no suggestion of this in the text. Rather, his honour as the king requires him to do his duty, and there is no way in which the Curse can be avoided. His decision is already made. The audience, which knows that curses in Greek tragedy, like dreams and prophecies, are almost always fulfilled, will doubtless agree. The Chorus, on the other hand, is right to maintain that it is madness to set out to kill his brother (for a different view, that Eteocles' decision to accept his destiny is both rational and correct, see Lawrence). And it is all the more chilling that he is able to justify his mad decision so rationally. This is Eteocles' tragedy. The scene ends (719) with his resigned words, 'you could not escape misfortunes when it is the gods who give them'.

After his departure the Chorus' ode on Apollo's oracle and Oedipus' Curse is in the right place. It is framed by the Erinys as the goddess who is bringing about their fulfilment. The expected Messenger arrives, and, in a brief exchange with the Chorus-leader, which has suffered from some disturbance to the text, reports that the city, the ship of state, has been saved, but that the Curse has indeed been fulfilled; Eteocles and Polyneices have killed each other, and they have divided the inheritance with the Scythian iron. In the rest of the play, as it is transmitted in the manuscripts, the Chorus begins to sing the lament which we might expect to provide the conclusion. But from 861-74 the Chorus, in anapaests, introduces to the audience Antigone and Ismene, the sisters of Polyneices and Eteocles, who then (875-1004) join with the Chorus in further lamentation. At every point the manuscripts are hopelessly confused and divided as to who the singer is. Finally a Herald arrives to announce the decision of the Council that Eteocles is to be given an honourable burial, but that the traitor Polyneices is to be left unburied for the dogs to eat. Antigone says that she will disobey the order. The play ends with anapaests from the Chorus, as one semi-chorus prepares to go off in one direction in Antigone's support, while the other semi-chorus departs with Ismene in the other direction in obedience to the city's command. It is widely, and probably rightly, held that much of this is a later interpolation, based on Sophocles' *Antigone* and Euripides' *Phoenician Women*. The likeliest view is that 861-74 and 1005 to the end should be deleted, thus removing Antigone and Ismene altogether, and that the lament at 875-1004 should be divided between the two semi-choruses. If this is correct, unless there is a fortunate papyrus find, we shall never know how the play originally ended – probably not at 1004, as we expect some reply to the question posed at 1002, 'where in the land shall we bury them?' But perhaps not much is missing.

There are further uncertainties at the end. At 745-9 the Chorus sang of how, according to the oracle, the city could be saved only if Laius did not have a son. Has not the oracle still to be fulfilled? Line 843 means more naturally that anxiety still remains for the city than that there is grief throughout the city. The myth knew of a continuation of the tragedy. The sons of the Seven grew up and, led by a son of Polyneices, avenged their fathers by invading and destroying Thebes, which was ruled by the son of Eteocles. Can it be coincidence that the word *epigonoi*, 'successors', the word always applied to the sons of the Seven, occurs at 903? It is not quite impossible that Aeschylus deliberately left his audience without a sense of closure. On the other hand at 828 the Chorus describes both Polyneices and Eteocles as 'childless', and the general impression (689-91, 953-60) is that with the death of the brothers the Curse has indeed died out.

Suppliants

The myth of the fifty daughters of Danaus is known in various versions from a large number of sources. Common to all of them is that, to avoid marriage with their fifty cousins, the sons of Aegyptus, they fled, with or without their father, from Egypt to their ancestral home in Argos. But the cousins pursued them, and forced the Danaids to marry them. On the wedding night forty-nine of the girls killed their bridegrooms, on the order of their father. Only Hypermestra spared her husband Lynceus, and they became the ancestors of the Argive royal family. In some versions Hypermestra was put on trial for disobeying her father, while in others it was the other Danaids who were tried for the murder. According to one account they were eventually married off to new suitors as prizes in a foot-race, while in a probably post-Aeschylean version they were punished in the underworld by being made to carry water for ever in perforated pitchers.

Suppliants belongs to a connected trilogy, of which the other two plays, *Aegyptii* and *Danaids*, have not survived; also lost is *Amymone*, the satyr-play, which presented the story of one of the Danaids, who was saved by Poseidon from the sexual assault of a satyr, only to succumb to the persuasion of the god. For many years the consensus has been that *Suppliants* was the first play in the trilogy, with *Aegyptii* and *Danaids* second and third respectively. Recently, however, there has been a move to place *Aegyptii* first and *Suppliants* second. The first play would then deal with the quarrel of Danaus and Aegyptus in Egypt, and provide the reason for the Danaids' flight, a matter which remains obscure in the surviving play. According to one version of the story an oracle had predicted that Danaus would be killed by his son-in-law, or more precisely by a son of Aegyptus. But this would mean that all of the main events of the story would have to be crowded into the third play. And, if the reason for the flight was to be found in the relationship between the two brothers, it is odd that in our play nothing is said of this, and that we are given a clear impression that the principal motivation is that of the Danaids themselves rather than of their father. It seems better to retain the usual view.

Suppliants presents the arrival of the girls and their father in Argos, the success of their appeal to king Pelasgus and the Argive people for asylum, and the arrival of a Herald sent ahead by the cousins, warning Pelasgus of war if he should refuse to surrender the girls. The fifty Danaids are represented by the usual twelve members of the Chorus, who form, in a non-technical sense, the protagonist of the play. For a tragedy to be concerned largely with the fortunes of a chorus, rather than of a mytho-logical hero, is very unusual. When the play was thought to be a very early one (see Intro. p. 7), most scholars, believing that Greek tragedy origi-nated in some kind of purely choral performance, imagined that the role of the Chorus in our play must have been typical of early tragedy. But there is more reason to suppose that in pre-Aeschylean one-actor tragedy, while the choral songs may have occupied a greater proportion of each play than in the later two-actor drama, its *dramatic* role was always secondary to that of the actor, with whose fortunes, not those of the Chorus, the tragedy is concerned. We should, therefore, look on *Suppli-ants* as a sophisticated and highly successful experiment in giving to a chorus a more dramatic role, one which Aeschylus tried again a few years later, though not so strikingly, in *Eumenides*, but which was not attempted by Sophocles or for the most part by Euripides, perhaps because with Sophocles' invention of the third actor, tragedy developed in a different direction. Few myths indeed would lend themselves to this treatment. There is no other play of Aeschylus in which a member of the Chorus in one play could emerge as a character in her own right in a later play of the trilogy, as Hypermestra evidently does in this one. The treatment of the Chorus here must have led to spectacular effects of staging. If the twelve members of the Chorus were accompanied throughout by an equal number of handmaids (see, however, p. 31), when the Herald tries to seize them he must have had enough men with him to make his attempt credible, while Pelasgus must have had sufficient soldiers to confront the Egyp-tians. No other surviving tragedy presents the excitement of an attempt to kidnap an entire chorus.

As in *Persians*, there is no actor-prologue. The play begins with the *parodos* of the Chorus, but, since this Chorus is the principal character, their entrance-song is much more dramatic than that of *Persians*, as the group of terrified, exotically dressed girls marches into the *orchestra* with anapaests which develop into lyrics. The *parodos* as a whole, with its frantic appeals to both Zeus and the land of Argos to save them from the *hybris* of their hated cousins, is as excited and emotional as those of *Seven against Thebes* and Euripides' later *Bacchae*; both of those plays, how-ever, open with a spoken prologue, whereas here the *parodos* begins the play. As often in Aeschylus, the first lines introduce themes that will be important for the development of the plot. The very first word is Zeus, patron god of suppliants. Both he and Pelasgus, the king of Argos, will have to be persuaded to support the girls. And at the outset (6-8) they make it clear that their flight from Argos is of their own volition. To remind Zeus that he has a particular obligation to help them, the Chorus tells the story of their ancestress Io, an Argive princess, who was loved by Zeus and turned into a cow by Zeus' wife Hera. Pursued by a gadfly, she eventually came to Egypt, where Zeus delivered his son Epaphus by breathing and touch (*epaphe*). Argos too should feel obliged to grant refuge to its own daughters. The theme of Io will recur in a remarkable fashion throughout the play. It is almost as if the Danaids see themselves as her reincarnation returning to her birthplace.

There can be no doubt that Aeschylus uses the *parodos* to engage the audience's sympathy on the side of the desperate and helpless Chorus. We want its appeals to succeed. But our response cannot be entirely straightforward. At 21-2, when the girls draw attention to the wool-wreathed suppliant branches which they are 'carrying in their hands', they use a word which often means 'daggers'. An audience that knows the story may look ahead to the brutal murder of their bridegrooms, and may feel that the girls are not as helpless as they seem. They express their confidence that Zeus will cast down their hated cousins, but at the same time they have to admit (89-90) that his ways are hard to understand. At 29-36 (cf. 528-30) they pray that he may sink their cousins' ship before it reaches Argos, but later in the play (734-5, 744, 1045-6) they will learn that he has not granted this request. Is Zeus really on their side? The *parodos* ends with a threat that, if their appeal should be unsuccessful, they will turn instead to the other Zeus, i.e. Hades, the god of the underworld; they will hang themselves, and will thus bring dishonour upon him for his failure to honour his own son Epaphus. We may feel some uneasiness at this attempt to threaten the supreme god. Their supplication is in danger of turning into an act of violence.

The first episode begins in a fairly leisurely fashion. Danaus, who has probably entered with the Chorus, and who is standing on a mound which contains an altar with the images of various gods (cf. the setting of *Seven against Thebes*) reports that he can see chariots approaching. In a long speech he advises his daughters on their behaviour. Since the Chorus is the principal character in the play, Danaus is not given very much to do, and there is little interaction in this play between the two actors. What matters is the relationship between the Chorus and Pelasgus, not that between Danaus and Pelasgus. Danaus' main role is to encourage and to advise, to offer the kind of conventional moralising that in normal Greek tragedies is put into the mouth of the Chorus, and thus to provide a change of mood. He may well be given a bigger part later in the trilogy. With the arrival of Pelasgus, accompanied by soldiers (it is unclear whether he comes on to the stage in his chariot), there begins a long movement in which the pace gradually increases until the climax is reached when the king finally decides to grant the Danaids' appeal for asylum. After a long speech in which Pelasgus introduces himself to the Chorus, he naturally wants to know the identity of the girls, but it takes some time before they can persuade him that they are Greeks and of Argive ancestry. They at least *look* to Pelasgus like exotic barbarians, and we should not forget that if their ancestry makes them Greek so too does it make their brutal barbarous cousins.

The pace quickens as we move into the stichomythia, the line-by-line question-and-answer dialogue at 291, in which the Chorus explains its descent from Io. It becomes still faster as the subject suddenly switches to the reason for the Danaids' flight. We may feel a moment of unease when Pelasgus asks whether the cousins may not have a right to marry them, and the Chorus avoids giving him a direct reply. More worrying, however, is Pelasgus' immediate realisation that, if he grants the appeal, he is likely to involve his country in war with the sons of Aegyptus. From the beginning of the play we have accepted that the Chorus is the centre of dramatic interest, but at this point we begin to understand that the fate of Pelasgus is to be not much less important. Aeschylus probably follows the version of the story in which Pelasgus is killed in a war in which Argos is defeated by the Egyptians, and Danaus succeeds him as king. Pelasgus therefore has his own tragedy, and it is interwoven with that of the Chorus. Our sympathies are divided; we want the Danaids to be granted asylum, but we do not want this exemplary king or the people whom he represents to suffer for it. In *Persians* Xerxes and Persia shared the same double tragedy, but here what appears to be salvation for the one party means tragedy for the other.

As the stichomythia ends, the Chorus warns Pelasgus against incurring the wrath of Zeus, the patron god of suppliants, and the pace again accelerates as we move into an *epirrhematikon*, an excited exchange in which the Chorus sings in the emotional dochmiac metre, while Pelasgus speaks in the normal iambic metre. For the first time in surviving Greek tragedy we see a character agonising over a decision. It is not Pelasgus' fault that he is in this situation, but it *is* his responsibility to choose between two courses of action, either of which is liable to be disastrous. He tries indeed to disclaim the responsibility; 'I would not make the decision without the people, even if I had (or 'even though I have'; the Greek is ambiguous) the power to do so' (398-9). Argos seems to have a constitutional democracy, in which the power is somehow shared between king and people. There is no need to try to relate this to the real historical Argos or to the political situation in Athens in the 460s. What matters is that the necessity for a double decision marks the magnitude of the dilemma, and that an audience, most of which was in favour of democracy, would feel sympathy for a king who consulted his people. In any case, since both Pelasgus and the people will suffer the consequences of the decision, the latter through the war and perhaps because of the pollution caused by the murder of the cousins, it is entirely appropriate that both should be involved in that decision.

Throughout all this the Chorus, rightly or probably wrongly, insists that Pelasgus has the power to act alone, and continues mercilessly to build up the pressure. At 438 the king sums up his dilemma in a longer speech: 'there can be no resolution that does not involve pain' (442). In a brief stichomythia the Chorus plays the same trump card that it has used on Zeus in the *parodos*: if Pelasgus rejects their appeal the girls will hang themselves on the images of the gods, and thereby bring pollution on the city. They are equally unscrupulous in their dealings with both god and man. Pelasgus finally concedes; 'I must', he says, 'respect the anger of Zeus god of suppliants' (478). The language is that of someone who tries to persuade himself that it is not his fault because he has no choice. But what he really means is that the pressure to choose A seems to him to be stronger than the pressure to choose B. The choice remains his. The episode ends with the departure of Pelasgus and Danaus for the city, where the assembly will be asked to ratify the decision that the king has made.

The Chorus' terror at being left alone suddenly reminds us that the cousins are on their way, and it is even suggested that they may arrive before Danaus and Pelasgus can return. But, having aroused our fears, Aeschylus immediately diverts our attention from them by giving to the Chorus an ode which is devoted to the wanderings of Io on her flight from Argos to Egypt. It all ended happily for Io, when Zeus released her from her sufferings. The girls are confident that Zeus, from whom they are descended, will do the same for them. They seem to forget that it was Zeus who caused Io's troubles in the first place, and it is slightly odd that, while they reject marriage for themselves, they celebrate the birth of Io's son. Danaus returns, and, in a very short episode, informs the Chorus that Pelasgus has had no difficulty in persuading the Argive assembly to give asylum to the refugees. The first movement of the play has thus come to a successful conclusion, and all the tension relaxes as the Chorus sings an ode of thanksgiving that is closer to the conventional tragic ode than any of its other songs. It takes the form of a prayer of blessings for the city – that it may be spared the horrors of foreign or civil war, and of plague and disease, that the crops and livestock may flourish, that Artemis may watch over women in childbirth, that happy songs may be heard in the land, and that the city may be well governed and honour the gods. The prayer may be conventional, and it certainly marks a moment of equilibrium, but we may note one or two paradoxes: the prayer for the avoidance of war is being uttered by those who will themselves bring war on Argos, and the prayer for easy childbirth by those who themselves reject marriage. But for the most part our thoughts are turned away from what is going to happen next. There is therefore a dramatic change of mood and a sudden shock when Danaus, in a scene that mirrors his announcement of the arrival of Pelasgus, and from the same position on the mound, reports that he can see the cousins' ship entering the harbour. After a further excited epirrhematic exchange between the panic-stricken Chorus, once more singing in emotional dochmiacs, and their father who, in more prosaic iambics, offers ineffective reassurance, Danaus departs to fetch help, leaving his daughters to face their enemies.

A song from the terrified Chorus, in which it strongly expresses its desire to die rather than submit to marriage, is rudely interrupted by the arrival on stage of an Egyptian Herald, sent ahead by the cousins, accompanied by his men (see p. 26). The scene is the earliest on-stage confrontation of enemies in extant tragedy, and its violence is unparalleled. In Sophocles' *Oedipus at Colonus* Antigone is carried off by Creon and his guards, but here it is an entire chorus that is in danger. Some have thought that the Herald's soldiers, as a secondary chorus, sing against the main Chorus in the lyrics from 825-71. More probably the singing role is given to the Herald alone, and it is certainly he who speaks the iambics at 873-5, 882-4, and 893-4, while the Danaids respond in lyrics. Although the text at this point is very corrupt, it seems that the Herald's barbarism is reflected in his use of exotic-sounding foreign words. It is unclear whether the threat of physical force is actually fulfilled, but certainly any doubts that we may have had about the Danaids' attitude and behaviour are now forgotten. The Herald is totally repulsive, and we may take it that those whom he represents will be equally so. The sudden arrival of Pelasgus is as welcome to the audience as it is to the Chorus. In an only slightly less excited stichomythia he routs the Herald, who departs with threats of the war that is bound to follow.

The play ends more quietly. Pelasgus tells the Chorus that it is time for it to go into the city, where it will have a choice of lodgings. The girls prepare for departure, each, if we are to believe the single manuscript, accompanied by her handmaid. But there is much to be said for Taplin's deletion of 977-9 as a later addition. The sudden appearance of the twelve servants at this point would be pointless, and it seems improbable that they have been present in the *orchestra* from the beginning of the play. Danaus returns, and in a long speech advises his daughters on how to behave inside the city; in particular they must do nothing to attract the attention of strange men. He too explains that they will be able to choose between accommodation provided by the city and rooms in the royal palace. Probably the significance of this will become apparent later in the trilogy; if they murder their cousins inside the palace, they will be killing their guests, which will make their crime even more serious. McCall (see also Rosenmeyer) maintains that the sung Finale is divided between two semi-choruses of Danaids, while other (improbable) suggestions are that the division is between Danaus or Hypermestra and the Chorus. Most scholars rightly believe that it is between the Danaid Chorus and a secondary Chorus; for some this comprises the handmaids or Argive women but much the likeliest view is that it is the Argive bodyguard given to Danaus by Pelasgus (traditionally the first step for someone who aspires to tyranny). It is disturbing that at the very end of the play this new voice warns the others against offending Aphrodite, goddess of love and sex, and reminds them that the future is uncertain. The main Chorus agrees that it cannot tell the mind of Zeus. So there is no closure at the end, and the next play in the trilogy is already being prepared.

Two questions also remain unanswered. Why do the Danaids refuse to marry their cousins, and do they hate all men or only the sons of Aegyptus? It is easy to cite passages which support both of these alternatives. As for the reason for their hatred, we have seen (see p. 25) that for some scholars all was explained in an earlier play. But there is not a word of that in *Suppliants*. There is no evidence in the text that the Danaids are devotees of the virgin goddess Artemis, and thus vowed to chastity. Nor is there any good reason to suppose either that the audience sympathises with the Danaids for rejecting marriage with their cousins as being incestuous, or conversely that it disapproves of them for refusing a marriage which for a fifth-century Athenian audience was not only permitted but even obligatory in the case of an heiress on the death of her father. The simile of the doves and falcons, of bird eating bird, at 223-9 has nothing to do with incest. The point is that the *hybris* of the cousins is all the worse because it is aimed at members of the same family. At 37-9 the Chorus claims that *themis* ('right', unwritten law) prevents the marriage. It may mean that the sons of Aegyptus have no right yet to marry them because their father is still alive. More probably they believe that it is wrong simply because their suitors are violent and they do not wish it. Perhaps that should be sufficient for us too. It remains disturbing that when Pelasgus suspects that right may be on the side of their cousins (see p. 28) they do not give him a direct answer. It may be that all will become clear at the end of the trilogy, but it is also possible that Aeschylus will leave the question unanswered. Tragedy is not required to solve all problems. Pelasgus' death and the accession of Danaus to the throne probably take place before the second play begins. The sons of Aegyptus probably form the Chorus, whose view of *hybris* may turn out to be very different from that of the Danaids. The murder is most likely to have taken place between the second and third plays, but it is idle to speculate on what happened next. Some favour a trial of Hypermestra for defying her father, others a trial of the others for murdering their husbands (see p. 25); and indeed there need not have been a trial at all. Finally, the trilogy may have looked towards a happier future. In a fragment of *Danaids* we find Aphrodite describing the fertilising power of rain on the earth in terms of sexual love and marriage. This seems to indicate that somehow the Danaids were persuaded to accept a voluntary marriage with new husbands, and that harmony is restored at the end.

The Oresteia
(i) Agamemnon

The *Oresteia* is the only surviving trilogy in which all three plays are connected with one another in their subject-matter, rather in the manner of a modern three-act play; at the same time each has its own independent dramatic unity. The lost satyr-play *Proteus* was also connected, in that it dealt with the visit of Agamemnon's brother Menelaus to Egypt on his return voyage from the Trojan War. *Agamemnon* is by far the longest play of Aeschylus to survive, and the trilogy as a whole is generally regarded as being the richest in the profundity of its tragic thinking and in the complexity of its imagery and its dramatic structure.

Agamemnon begins with a monologue delivered by a minor character who will not be seen again in the play. He is a watchman, posted probably on the roof of the stage-building, which represents the palace of Agamemnon at Argos, and his role is to introduce us to the situation at the start of the play. He has been watching for the beacon that will announce the fall of Troy and the end of the war, and he is becoming weary. Indeed in the opening line of the play he prays to the gods for a release from his troubles. The first hint that by 'troubles' he means more than his physical discomfort comes at line 11 with his enigmatic reference to the 'woman with a heart that thinks like a man', i.e. Clytaemestra, Agamemnon's wife. Gender roles will be an important theme throughout this trilogy. But then, in the middle of his speech, the Watchman sees the beacon and his misgivings turn to joy. The symbolism of light and darkness will pervade the trilogy. Here the light is made visible to the Watchman, though not to the audience. The plot of the play has already started to develop. The Watchman prepares to go off to inform Clytaemestra of the good news. But before he leaves he remarks that there are matters about which he will keep silent: a big ox is on his tongue, but 'the house itself, if it could find a voice, would speak most clearly'. So we are introduced to the house of Agamemnon with all its dark secrets, the house which has been described as almost an actor in the drama. The prologue thus presents a movement, from foreboding to joy and then back to foreboding, that will be mirrored in the play as a whole; the joy will never last.

The *parodos* (entrance-song) of the Chorus of Argive elders is by far the longest in surviving Greek tragedy. Until 104 it declaims in recitative anapaests as it marches into the *orchestra*, and from then until 257 it sings in lyric metres. It has not yet heard the news of victory, but wonders why it has seen altars blazing with the celebratory offerings of Clytaemestra. When the *parodos* ends more than 200 lines later it may seem that the action has not advanced at all. Instead, the Chorus has taken us back to the past, to the departure ten years ago of the Greek expedition for Troy. In particular, it tells us of the cross-winds at Aulis which prevented the expedition from sailing until Agamemnon, to propitiate the goddess Artemis, sacrificed his daughter Iphigeneia. No other passage in the play has been more discussed than this. The anger of Artemis is left unexplained by Aeschylus, but it seems that she, the protectress of the young of all wild creatures, objects to the sacrifice of innocent lives that the war will entail. Yet it is Zeus himself who sends out Agamemnon on the expedition to punish Paris Alexander for robbing Menelaus of his wife Helen, and the Trojans for protecting the malefactors. The sacrifice of his daughter will be the first offence for which Agamemnon will be rightly punished. And yet it seems that he did it in obedience to Zeus' command. Where does the responsibility lie? The Chorus sings of how he went under the yoke-strap of necessity. Some have thought that this means that it was all fated. Rather, the sense is that Agamemnon, through no fault of his own, found himself in a position in which he was forced to make a choice between two evils, between abandoning the expedition and sacrificing his daughter. But he *was* responsible for the choice that he made. Perhaps too we may think of the person who says 'I had no choice' when he really means that the pressure to do A was stronger than the pressure to do B (see p. 29). Anyway, the Chorus clearly does hold Agamemnon to be responsible. It is full of misgivings, which are strengthened by the thought that, although commanded by Zeus, the war was all for the sake of a promiscuous woman (62; cf. 225-6). Three times we hear the ominous refrain, 'Sing woe, sing woe, but let the good prevail', the kind of wishful thinking that will be uttered by most of the characters in the play. When at 153-5 the Chorus has a vivid picture of child-avenging Anger as the deceitful housekeeper in the palace, we think of Clytaemestra, the literal keeper of the house. The Chorus tries to reassure itself with the thought that Zeus has laid it down that learning comes through suffering (*pathei* 177; others, more weakly, translate 'experience'). But is the stress on the learning or on the suffering, and who is it that learns? All of this happened ten years ago, but it is as if we were back there at Aulis with Agamemnon agonising over his dilemma. In a technical sense the action of the play begins with the Watchman on the roof, but through the Chorus' song it really begins at Aulis. And we look ahead in dread to the future.

It is not clear whether Clytaemestra has entered with the Chorus, or at 83, or whether she does so only at the end. She now announces to the Chorus that the war has been won. The Chorus-leader, however, is sceptical; perhaps the queen has been dreaming. To prove that her report is true Clytaemestra describes at length the chain of beacons that has brought the news all the way from Troy to Argos. Her speech is full of flashing light and fire, as the message passes from one beacon to the next, with the whole speech embodying the symbolism of the light of victory and salvation. It is as if all Greece is on fire and blazing with joy. But, when she comes to the final link in the chain, we are reminded that fire can also be a destructive force; the beacon that 'swooped down' on the house of the sons of Atreus at Argos is described in language appropriate to a lightning-flash or a thunderbolt. And it descends from the first fire in the chain, the one that destroyed the city of Troy. In a second speech Clytaemestra gives an imaginative account of the army which has now been released from its troubles at Troy. She ends with a warning: to ensure a safe return it must behave piously towards the Trojan gods and not ravage what should not be ravaged. 'Such is the account that you hear from me a [mere] woman' (348), she concludes with mock self-deprecation.

The Chorus, now convinced, begins the expected song of joyous victory. Zeus has rightly punished Paris for his crime against the laws of hospitality in stealing Menelaus' wife, just as everyone is punished who 'tramples on the grace of things that should not be touched' (the significance of this phrase will become apparent later). The mood, however, gradually changes. A beautiful description of the sorrow of Menelaus, who lost his wife, leads to the more recent sorrows of all those who lost their loved ones in the war; instead of the men only ashes return. The people are therefore angry, and the gods too take note of those who are responsible for the deaths of many. It is dangerous to be too successful. By the end of the song the Chorus, unable now to face the consequences of victory, takes refuge in wishful thinking: perhaps the war is not over after all. It is only a woman who has reported it, and women are unreliable. So the male Chorus, so scornful of female irrationality, itself behaves irrationally.

Its refusal to face the truth is rudely shattered by the arrival of a Herald, who reports that Troy has indeed fallen, and that Agamemnon is on his way 'bringing light in darkness' (522); he deserves a suitable welcome. But what is a suitable welcome for the man who sacrificed his own daughter, who is responsible for so many deaths, and who, as the Herald now reports, has destroyed the altars and sanctuaries of the gods? We remember Clytaemestra's warning. In a further speech the Herald recalls the miseries of life in camp at Troy, but now they are all over. Clytaemestra enjoys her triumph over the Chorus; the men were wrong, and she, the woman, was right to believe the beacons. She sends the Herald back to Agamemnon to tell him of the faithful wife who is waiting for him at home. There is considerable uncertainty about Clytaemestra's entries and exits in this play, but it seems likely that she goes back into the palace at 614, leaving the Chorus-leader to question the Herald about the fate of Menelaus. His reply is ominous. A great storm scattered the fleet on the homeward voyage, and only Agamemnon's ship has returned safely. Things have already begun to go wrong. When we shall see Agamemnon we shall know that he is alone and unprotected, and we may suspect that the gods have saved him only for a worse fate at home.

Left alone in the *orchestra* the Chorus' song begins with a beautiful description of Helen as she set off with Paris, and came to Troy, where she was welcomed with a wedding hymn. But that soon turned for the Trojans to a dirge. In the fable a lion-cub was brought up as a family pet, but when it grew up it caused havoc in the household. So when Helen came to Troy she turned out to be an Erinys, an avenging Fury. The thought of Troy's destruction leads the Chorus to speculate about divine punishment for *hybris*: it is impious deeds, not prosperity, that, having led to further acts of *hybris*, especially in prosperous houses, are duly punished. No doubt the Chorus is still thinking of Paris and the Trojans, but for the audience it all applies to Agamemnon, the man who sacrificed his daughter, who lost so many men in a war fought for the sake of a promiscuous woman, and who committed sacrilege at Troy. As we wait for Agamemnon's arrival we know that he is doomed, and, as the song ends, we shudder as we see him entering in his chariot. Beside him he has Cassandra, the prophetess daughter of King Priam, whom Agamemnon has brought home as his concubine. The audience notices her, but it will be some time before Aeschylus reveals the part that she is to play.

The Chorus' greeting to its king is lukewarm. It never really approved of the war, it says, fought for the sake of a mere woman, but still it is glad that Agamemnon won. It hints that not everyone in Argos is sympathetic to the king. In his lengthy response Agamemnon shows himself to be a master of pomposity, as he thanks the gods who, along with himself, have won the war, fought for the sake of a woman. He takes note of the Chorus' warning, but has no doubt that he can apply the appropriate medicine or surgery where it is required. He ends with the usual wishful thinking: may his victory be a lasting one. Clytaemestra is not present to greet her husband. Some have thought that his failure even to mention her charac-terises him as unfeeling. Rather, Aeschylus keeps us waiting for the relationship between husband and wife to be presented, and when it comes she will take the initiative. As Agamemnon prepares to dismount from his chariot at 854 and to go into the palace, the great door opens and there stands Clytaemestra blocking the way. So far she is the only character who has used the door. As Taplin says, the palace is Clytaemestra's domain, and no one can go through the door except on her terms.

At first she addresses not her husband but the Chorus. And, as he is a master of pomposity, so she is a mistress of hypocrisy. 'I shall not be ashamed', she says (856-7), 'to tell you of my husband-loving ways', but the adjective may equally be translated as 'man-loving', and we think of Aegisthus her paramour. 'It is a terrible misfortune for a wife (or "woman") to sit alone at home without her husband (or "a man"; she has not been without Aegisthus)'. If all the reports of his death had been true, Agamemnon would have been like a net full of holes. Later she will find a more sinister use for a 'net'. Eventually she turns to address her husband, first to explain the absence of their son Orestes (Aeschylus already looks forward to the next play), and then to dwell at length on her own misery during her husband's absence. But all that is over. In a cascade of overblown metaphors she describes the joy of a house when its lord and master returns safely to it. Without a break, in the middle of a line (905), she introduces something new, as she invites Agamemnon to step down from his chariot, and orders her servants to lay out crimson fabrics so that Justice may lead Agamemnon over them into 'the house which he did not expect to see'; i.e. he thought that he would never return home, but the audience may think of the house of Hades, which he certainly does not expect to see.

So the episode ends with Clytaemestra persuading her husband to walk over the fabrics into the palace, which is her domain. This is often described as the 'carpet'-scene, but carpets were unknown in fifth-century Greece, and carpets are meant to be walked on, whereas it is clear that what Agamemnon treads underfoot is something that only gods should walk on; to say the least, he is wasting the house's wealth. We may recall Paris who was punished for trampling on things that should have been untouched (see p. 35). He knows that he will attract the gods' anger for doing it, but he is no match for the persuasive powers of his wife, especially in the brief stichomythia at 931-43, where he gives the wrong answer to all her questions. Three different kinds of symbolism are involved. First, we have *heard* so far of all the various acts of *hybris* which Agamemnon has committed, but now for the first time we *see* him committing *hybris*. It is not *because* of it that he will fall. Rather, this walking on the fabrics symbolises all that has gone before. Secondly, the scene symbolises all that, for a fifth-century audience, is wrong with the relationship between the sexes in the palace at Argos. As the woman earlier triumphed over the male Chorus, so she now with her manipulative language triumphs easily over the male Agamemnon. And thirdly, the dark red fabrics streaming out through the door of the palace are the colour of dried blood (therefore not 'purple', as the word is often translated), the blood of Agamemnon which is about to be shed inside. It is over this that he walks, having had his boots removed in a vain attempt to avert the anger of the gods. Probably the servants roll up the fabrics behind him. As Goward says, he will not need them again as he will not be walking out. Before he goes, he introduces Cassandra to his wife, and asks her to treat her gently; nobody likes to bear the yoke of slavery. The next scene is thus prepared.

We are, however, kept waiting for it while the Chorus sings a gloomy song. It does not know what is going to happen, but it is vaguely uneasy. Other evils can be averted, but when blood is shed it cannot be recalled (a recurring motif in this trilogy). The audience waits for Agamemnon's death-shrieks, or for a messenger to report his death. But we have almost forgotten Cassandra, who is still standing silent in the chariot. She can hardly remain there until the end of the play. It is therefore not a complete surprise when Clytaemestra emerges from the palace to summon her indoors to share in the sacrifices. From the queen's point of view it is a good omen when a victim goes quietly and willingly to be sacrificed. The Chorus-leader urges her to submit to the necessity of putting on the yoke of slavery. Cassandra, however, declines even to speak, and Clytaemestra has to return through the door alone. It is the first time that she has been defeated, and it has taken another woman to do it. By this time we have probably concluded that Cassandra's part is to be a non-speaking one. The scream that she now emits is, therefore, particularly shocking. Her role is to prophesy the death of Agamemnon and her own, and, so that she may prove her credibility as a prophetess, to reveal her knowledge of the earlier events in the story of this unhappy family. Of all the characters in the play she alone understands and can show us the indissoluble connection of past, present and future time. She recalls Thyestes' adultery with the wife of Atreus, Agamemnon's father (1192-3), and with her vision (1095-8; cf. 1217-22) of infants served up for their father's meal the audience would instantly recognise the reference to the cannibal feast prepared for Thyestes by his brother. Thyestes cursed Atreus and all his family (1600-2). For the first time in the play we learn that the question of Agamemnon's responsibility is even more complex than we had thought. He has committed his own offences, but he has also inherited the curse. As for the future, Cassandra presents a vivid picture of a woman murdering her husband in his bath (1107-11, 1125-9). The cloak that she will use to trap her husband is described as a net, and at 1116 Clytaemestra herself is a net.

The Chorus finds it impossible to believe her. According to the myth Apollo loved Cassandra, and bestowed on her the gift of uttering prophecies that were always true. But, because she refused his sexual advances, he cursed her with the inability to persuade anyone that they *were* true. Aeschylus turns this element of the story to his own dramatic purpose. This male Chorus, which earlier refused to accept the truth when told it by the other woman Clytaemestra, does not *want* to believe what Cassandra is saying because it cannot face it. The first part of the scene comprises a remarkable *epirrhematic* exchange which begins with the excited Cassandra singing in largely lyric verses to which the Chorus-leader responds with spoken iambics. This is a total reversal of the normal practice in which an actor speaks while the Chorus sings. But it is perfectly adapted to this situation in which all the emotion is displayed by the actor while the uncomprehending Chorus replies stolidly in the more prosaic language of speech. Eventually even the Chorus is caught up in the excitement, and begins to sing, largely in emotional dochmiacs. The second part of the scene, from 1178, becomes calmer, as the Chorus-leader and Cassandra both switch to spoken iambics, in which Cassandra describes her memorable vision of a chorus of Erinyes (Furies), which has drunk human blood and is refusing to leave the house in which it is singing its unharmonious song. She also prophesies that one day Orestes will return home to avenge his father, and that a woman will die for a woman, a man for a man, thereby preparing a transition to the next play in the trilogy. By the end of the scene the Chorus has come to understand that something is far wrong, but it still cannot grasp exactly what is going to happen or how soon. It can accept that Cassandra will die (for it is not emotionally involved with her), but when she tells them bluntly (1246), 'I say that you will see the death of Agamemnon', it can only advise her to mind her language, and it then merely expresses the hope that it will not happen, and finally asks 'what *man* is preparing this grievous thing?' So Cassandra departs into the palace to her death.

After a few words from the worried Chorus we hear at last the death-shrieks of Agamemnon from behind the *skene*. In some thirty lines of stichomythia the Chorus, very unusually, divides up into individuals who debate in spoken iambics what to do. Some are for rushing into the palace to protect their king, while others are more cautious, and in the end the Chorus decides to wait for further information. By dramatic convention a chorus is not allowed to enter the *skene* or to interfere in the action to that extent. But, in dramatic terms, everything that we have seen of the Chorus earlier in the play has prepared us for its ineffectiveness now. By the time that the discussion has ended it is anyway too late and there is Clytaemestra once more dominating the door, standing with a sword over the bodies of Agamemnon and Cassandra and the bath in which she has murdered her husband. The audience sees also the net-like robe in which she trapped him. The tableau is evidently presented on the *ekkyklema*, the trolley which could be pushed out through the central door to reveal an indoor scene to the audience.

Clytaemestra is at her most magnificent. Far from being ashamed of her deed, she revels in it. She has ensured that Agamemnon was unable to leap out of her net, the net of her deceit and the net that is the robe. The third stroke with her sword she compares, with superb blasphemy, to the third libation that was customarily offered to Zeus the Saviour. When she was showered with Agamemnon's blood it gave her as much pleasure as the corn receives when it is showered by the rain that comes from Zeus. The blasphemy is shocking, as is the perversion of the idea of life-giving rain to an image of violent death.

In the ensuing quarrel between Clytaemestra and the Chorus the queen attempts to justify her action on the grounds that Agamemnon deserved to die because he killed her daughter Iphigeneia, 'my dearest birth-pangs' (1417; cf. 1525-9). We know that she is a practised hypocrite, but there is no good reason to doubt the sincerity of this claim. One may have some sympathy too for her complaint that he has brought home Cassandra to be his concubine. It is expressed in language which suggests that he made a habit of this kind of thing when he was at Troy. But she spoils it somewhat by her boast that she will never be afraid as long as Aegisthus is around to light the fire in her hearth. We have perhaps forgotten her own adultery with Aegisthus, which provides a less acceptable motive for her killing of her husband, and in any case the idea that this powerful woman relies on the protection of any man does not ring true. We may suspect also that she has a further motive, which she does not acknowledge directly, the desire to continue wielding the power at Argos.

However, as the scene develops there is a gradual change of mood. Her claim that the ancient spirit of vengeance has taken her form leads to understandable bafflement on the part of the Chorus, as it tries to grapple with the complex problem of motivation and shared responsibility. It fears that there is more trouble still to come, and reminds Clytaemestra that 'as long as Zeus remains on his throne it remains that the doer must suffer' (1563-4). And, in a splendid metaphor, it declares that 'the house is glued to ruin' (1566). Clytaemestra agrees, and hopes that it might be possible to negotiate an agreement with the *daemon* (destiny) of the house to go away and trouble some other family. It seems that, even for Clytaemestra, joy and self-confidence cannot last, but must give way to anxiety and foreboding. But at this point, just as she and the Chorus appear to be reaching some kind of understanding, Aegisthus suddenly appears, unusually late in a play for the entry of a major character. As he threatens the Chorus and prepares to yoke the disobedient and to enjoy the tyranny which he will exercise he is utterly repulsive. Yet even he, as the son of Thyestes and the sole survivor of the cannibal-feast, can claim to have justice on his side. The Chorus is not impressed. It calls him a woman, and taunts him with having in cowardly fashion left it to his mistress to murder Agamemnon; to which he can reply only that deceit was more appropriate for a woman. The Chorus prepare to take up their staves for a fight with Aegisthus' bodyguard armed with their swords. It was no match for the woman Clytaemestra, who needed no bodyguard, but it is quite ready now to take action against a man. Ironically it is Clytaemestra who seems to be genuinely weary of bloodshed, and tells the Chorus to go home. There is a further reminder from the Chorus-leader that Orestes may return to put things right. In the last line of the play Clytaemestra refers to the authority that she and Aegisthus will now wield jointly in the house, and they leave the stage together. The play thus ends in deadlock. Evil seems to have triumphed, but there is no real happiness for anyone. And already the next play is prepared. In its first line Orestes will refer enigmatically to the authority of his dead father Agamemnon in the underworld, the power that will help him to regain the authority at Argos.

The Oresteia
(ii) Libation Bearers

Libation Bearers, like *Agamemnon*, begins with a prologue that consists entirely in a monologue, but here the speaker is not a minor character but the protagonist, in which respect we may compare it with the beginning of *Suppliants*. In the single manuscript that contains the play the opening of the prologue is missing, and the first nine lines have been restored from a quotation in Aristophanes' *Frogs* and from ancient commentaries on Pindar and Euripides' *Alcestis*. It is unlikely that much more has been lost.

Agamemnon ended with Clytaemestra and Aegisthus preparing to enjoy the exercise of *kratos* (power) in Agamemnon's palace. *Libation Bearers* begins with the return from exile of Orestes, who at Agamemnon's tomb prays to Hermes as the guardian of his father's *kratos*. The language is ambiguous. The *kratos* might be that of Hermes' father, Zeus, who under his title *Saviour* (2) was offered the third libation after Athenian dinner-parties (see p. 40). More probably Orestes refers to the power of his own father Agamemnon, who, though dead, is still a mighty figure in the underworld. Hermes, to whose chthonic associations line 1 explicitly refers, is to ensure that Agamemnon's power may enter into his son, so that he may recover the *kratos* that Clytaemestra and Aegisthus are now exercising at Argos. Orestes has come home to avenge his father's murder, and his prayer develops at the end of the prologue into a prayer to Zeus himself to help him. He has dedicated a lock of his hair to the river Inachus which has nurtured him, as a token of his reaching manhood. He is therefore young and inexperienced, and his vengeance will be the first act of that manhood. His motives, unlike those of Clytaemestra, are pure, and the note of hope with which the play begins contrasts with the end of the preceding play. Orestes does not say explicitly that he intends to kill his mother, and at this early stage Aeschylus does not encourage his audience to consider that this is what the vengeance will entail.

The note of hope, however, is not the only, or indeed the predominant, one. The *skene*, which represents the palace of Agamemnon, is still present at the back of the stage, and we can hardly forget the dark secrets which it concealed in the earlier play. We know that, if he is to avenge his father's murder, Orestes must eventually pass through the door into the palace. But throughout the first half of the play our attention is focused, not on the *skene*, but on Agamemnon's tomb, with all its funereal associations, on which Orestes offers a further lock of hair to his dead father. The tomb is evidently some kind of temporary construction, perhaps at the centre of the *orchestra*, like that of Darius in *Persians*. We are to be kept waiting for Orestes' entrance into the palace.

As the prologue of *Agamemnon* was interrupted by the Watchman's sight of the beacon, so here Orestes breaks off at 10 to announce the arrival (probably by a side-passage) of his sister Electra and the Chorus, carrying the libations which give the play its name. The action has already begun. The black dress of mourning to which he calls our attention reinforces the sense of gloom. As the prologue ends Orestes introduces to the audience his friend Pylades, and together they withdraw into hiding so as to observe unseen the arrival of the newcomers – the earliest known example of what was later to become a stage-convention. Pylades says nothing, and the audience doubtless assumes that he is to be a non-speaking extra in the play.

The female Chorus consists of prisoners of war. Despite many commentators, Aeschylus does not say that they were brought back from Troy by Agamemnon, and, as Sommerstein points out, their old age (171) is not consistent with their having been taken from their fathers' houses (76-7; i.e. as unmarried young women) only a few years earlier. What matters is that they are hostile to Clytaemestra, the 'impious woman' (46), and sympathetic to Electra. The *parodos* in effect takes the form of the ritual dirge which Agamemnon had been denied at his funeral. It is full of darkness, anger, fear and death, and prominence is given to two of the recurring themes of the trilogy, that justice may be delayed but will come in the end, and that blood once shed can never be recalled or washed away (see p. 38). The Chorus has been sent by Clytaemestra, who has had a nightmare, warning her of her husband's anger, and causing her to scream in terror in the night. The libations are intended to appease him. Only later shall we be informed of the details of the dream. For the moment we may appreciate the dramatic irony whereby the steps taken by Clytaemestra to appease her husband are likely to lead to the meeting of brother and sister at the tomb, and to the subsequent success of Orestes' plan to avenge his father. Dreams were believed to come from the underworld, and to be brought by Hermes. Orestes' prayer to that god at the beginning of the prologue has thus already been answered.

At the beginning of the first episode Electra, naturally reluctant to obey her mother's instructions, asks the Chorus-leader whether she should simply throw away the offerings. The Chorus-leader advises her to offer the libations but to accompany them with a prayer for vengeance on 'those responsible for the murder'. There is still no explicit reference to the intended murder of a mother by her son. Electra duly prays, in a prayer that parallels closely that of Orestes in the prologue. She too begins with chthonic Hermes. When she asks that her brother may come home we know that her prayer too has already been answered, and we look forward to the joy of their coming reunion. When she prays (140-1) that she may be more chaste than her mother, we approve of her desire to behave as a proper woman should.

As the libations are poured on the tomb the Chorus sings a brief prayer to Agamemnon that an avenger might appear. Electra reports that she has found the lock of hair left by Orestes, and so the recognition scene begins. The hair resembles her own, and, though at first she realises that her brother may have *sent* it home, her hope that he may have brought it in person is beginning to prevail when, in the second stage of the recognition, her hope seems to be confirmed as she sees his footprint, and declares that it too is similar to her own. But now, when Orestes himself appears from his hiding-place, and she is actually confronted by her brother, she paradoxically refuses to believe that he really is Orestes, and it is only in the third stage, when he shows her the garment that he is wearing, woven and embroidered long ago by herself, that she is convinced and greets him joyously.

By the standards of later Greek recognition scenes this earliest example may seem in some respects naïve. Euripides indeed will make fun of it in his *Electra*. One may question whether the colour or texture of a lock of hair, or the size or proportions of a footprint, would be sufficient to reveal the identity of its owner, or why Orestes is still wearing the clothes which he wore as a small child when he was sent away from Argos. It is a mistake to look too hard for rational answers. Electra knows that only a member of the family would have left the offering on the tomb, and the audience knows that Orestes is in fact the owner of the hair. More important, we sympathise with Electra in her irrational changes of mood, which characterise her for the Greek audience as different from her mother Clytaemestra, the 'woman with a heart that thinks like a man' (see p. 33), and we wait happily for the recognition. For a moment we forget the gloom.

So far, Orestes and Electra have prayed separately to the gods. Now that they are happily united Orestes prays to Olympian Zeus on behalf of them both. He describes them as the orphaned offspring of an eagle father (Agamemnon) who died in the coils of a terrible viper (Clytaemestra)

(246-9). The enmity of the eagle and the snake was traditional. There was a belief that the female viper killed her partner while mating, and that the offspring of their union avenged their father by killing their mother as they bit their way out of her womb. The coils may suggest the robe in which Clytaemestra trapped Agamemnon in his bath. Orestes is the son both of the noble eagle and of the snake. The scene ends with a long speech in which Orestes describes how Apollo at Delphi had threatened him with the Erinyes, his father's avenging Furies, should he fail to avenge his father's death. But he makes it clear that, even without Apollo's command, he has his own motives for killing the murderers (plural; there is still no specific mention of his mother). The god and Orestes himself will share the responsibility for what he is about to do.

The *kommos* (see p. 16) that follows is one of the most remarkable lyric compositions in Greek tragedy. It is certainly the longest and the most complex in its structure. Shared by Orestes, Electra and the Chorus, each with separate singing parts, and by the Chorus-leader in recitative ana- paests, it purports to be an appeal to the dead Agamemnon to come and help his offspring avenge his murder. Sometimes we have the feeling that the angry soul of Agamemnon is still present in his tomb seeking revenge on his murderers (cf. 40-1). Sometimes it seems that he is far away in the underworld, and that it is Orestes who has to take the initiative. There is therefore much emphasis on ensuring that the ritual and the language are correct; for it is not easy to bridge the gap between the world of light and the darkness of the underworld. As it slowly progresses, the audience, especially those who had witnessed the evocation of Darius fourteen years earlier in *Persians*, must have wondered whether Agamemnon's ghost would actually be conjured up on the stage. It is more effective that he remains unseen, but that we have a sense of his power entering into Orestes, in answer to the latter's prayer at the beginning of the play.

From a dramatic point of view the *kommos* has a second purpose, to show us Orestes making his decision to kill his mother. Some scholars have doubted this, on the grounds that in the prologue he has already made it clear that he has come home to take revenge, and in the speech before the *kommos* he is already committed to obeying Apollo's command. But we are not to think of him making his decision on three separate occasions. Rather, Aeschylus presents the same decision in different but parallel ways. Lines 297-305 provide a transition from the command of Apollo to the *kommos* in which Apollo is not mentioned at all, and we see Orestes accepting the responsibility for his decision. Above all, it is here for the first time that he unequivocally declares his intention to kill his mother. We do not see him in an agony of indecision as to whether it can be right to do so. At first he simply refuses to face necessity. He takes refuge in irrational wishes for what might be, or what might have been, and in prayers to the gods to do the job for him, and it is the role of the Chorus, and especially of the Chorus-leader, to remind him that it is not wishes and prayers but action that is required. At the very beginning the Chorus-leader stresses one of the recurring themes of the trilogy, that the doer must suffer (313). The crucial moment comes at 435-7, as he finally commits himself to matricide: 'she will pay for dishonouring my father, by the help of the gods, and by the help of my own hands'. Gone is the vague plural ('the killers'), yet he still cannot bring himself to call Clytaemestra 'mother'.

With the *kommos* completed Orestes and Electra, in normal spoken iambics, make a final appeal to Agamemnon, reminding him of the shame of his death in the net-like robe. Then at last we hear from the Chorus-leader of the details of Clytaemestra's nightmare. She dreamed that she gave birth to a snake that drew blood along with milk from her breast when she suckled it. We remember 247-9 where Orestes was the offspring of the snake. His mother was right to be afraid, but she thought that, as in the earlier version of the story presented by the lyric poet Stesichorus, the dream portended an appearance of the dead Agamemnon himself. She did not know, but Orestes now recognises, that the snake would be her son, into whom the power of Agamemnon has entered. The episode ends with a speech in which Orestes outlines his plan for vengeance. Electra is to retire into the palace, and we shall not see her again. Sophocles and Euripides would later make her the protagonist of their versions of the story, but for Aeschylus her work is done. From now on all our concen-tration will be on Orestes. He and Pylades will come to the palace-door claiming to be Phocians. He envisages a situation in which they will be kept outside until Aegisthus is shamed into admitting them. If they find him sitting on Agamemnon's throne, Orestes will kill him with his sword. A scene of this kind is portrayed on various artistic representations from as early, probably, as the seventh century. But none of this will happen in *Libation Bearers*. Aeschylus is deliberately misleading his audience, so that he can surprise it later. More important, Orestes, in his preoccupation with Aegisthus, makes no plans for dealing with his mother. Once more our thoughts are diverted from the horror of matricide. Orestes and Pylades leave the stage by a side-passage to make their preparations, while Electra exits probably by the central door in the *skene* into the palace. It is the first time in the play that it has been used, and we are thus prepared for the refocusing that takes place during the following ode from tomb to palace. In his final words Orestes calls on 'this one' to supervise him in the coming contest. Commentators are divided as to whether 'this one' is Pylades, Agamemnon, Apollo (represented by a statue), or Hermes (represented by a statue). With the last of these the ring-composition with line 1 rounds off the first part of the play.

The Chorus in its ode sings of how, although there are many terrors in the natural world, nothing is worse than female passion, and of how Clytaemestra's wickedness surpasses that of women famous in mythology for the crimes that they committed within the family. As the ode began we were prepared for Orestes to confront and kill the male Aegisthus, but now our thoughts are turned instead to the female Clytaemestra. Is her death imminent? Again Aeschylus is teasing his audience. Orestes and Pylades duly enter and knock three times on the great central door of the palace. The Servant who responds probably remains unseen behind the door, as we wait to see who will open it. Orestes orders him to summon the one who wields authority in the house, a woman or, more fittingly, a man. So the uncertainty remains, until finally the door opens and it is Clytaemestra who stands there, as she stood in *Agamemnon* to greet her husband, still in apparent control of the entrance to the palace. If we expect Orestes to despatch her instantly we are to be surprised. The whole scene is framed by Clytaemestra's courteous offer of hospitality and its acceptance by Orestes. We may, however, shudder as she speaks of the things that are 'appropriate to this house' (669; cf. 714), especially as they include hot baths, and we remember what happened to Agamemnon in his bath. We also look ahead with misgivings to the murder of his hostess by a guest who has accepted her hospitality. In the preceding play the man was deceived by the woman, whereas here it is the other way round. Clytaemestra is completely taken in by Orestes' lying account of his own death. In her expressions of grief she may be displaying the hypocrisy that characterised her in *Agamemnon* (cf. 737-41 in this play), but there is no good reason here to deny her some maternal feelings. At the end even of *Agamemnon* she was genuinely weary of the bloodshed in the house. The scene ends with the departure of Clytaemestra, Orestes and Pylades through the central door into the palace, the two men being conducted by a servant towards the men's quarters inside.

After a brief anapaestic passage from the expectant Chorus, as it waits for Hermes to supervise Orestes' contest (see above), the door opens yet again, and we no doubt assume that a messenger will emerge to announce the death of Clytaemestra. Again Aeschylus surprises us. It is Cilissa, the old nurse of Orestes, sent by Clytaemestra to fetch Aegisthus who happens to be out of the palace. It seems after all that his death is to be presented first. The Nurse is a traditional character in this story, and Aeschylus uses her for three purposes. She is the ordinary decent person who loves Orestes for himself, not, as he is for Electra and the Chorus, as a potential avenger; secondly, by her reminiscences of the ordinary babyhood of the little boy who wet his 'nappies' she provides a grim contrast with the grown man, the first act of whose manhood will be to murder his mother; and thirdly, she provides a contrast also between the woman who really cared for Orestes as a child and the biological mother who gave birth to the snake. As she departs on her mission, the Chorus-leader asks her if Aegisthus is to bring his bodyguard, the bodyguard which, we may remember, he required at the end of *Agamemnon* in his confrontation with the Chorus (see p. 41). When the Nurse says yes, the Chorus-leader persuades her to change the message so that he will come alone and unprotected. It is highly unusual for a tragic chorus to influence so decisively the development of a plot.

While we await the arrival of Aegisthus the Chorus sings an ode, textually very corrupt, in which it prays to Zeus, the household gods (in this context perhaps the Erinyes), Apollo, and Hermes to grant Orestes success, and that he (or the house) may see the light of freedom after the veil of darkness. It looks forward to singing a song of celebration, and ends by encouraging Orestes to be as resolute when facing Clytaemestra as Perseus was when he confronted the Gorgon. It is, then, to Clytaemestra that our thoughts are finally turned, so that once more it comes as a surprise as we see Aegisthus coming up the side-passage on to the stage.

Aegisthus' appearance is very brief, and he is no more impressive a character than he was in *Agamemnon*. He wants to hear the news of Orestes from the stranger himself. The Chorus invites him to go into the palace to do so, and off he goes to his doom, after asserting cheerfully that there is no way in which the messenger could deceive him. After a brief anapaestic passage from the Chorus we hear his off-stage death cry, and immediately, as we approach the dramatic climax of the play, Aeschylus begins to prepare us for the killing that really matters. A servant emerges from the central door on his way to fetch Clytaemestra from the women's quarters. The door which he calls on to be opened can hardly be the same central door from which he has himself only just emerged, and it is unlikely that we are to imagine it off stage. Rather, we should accept the existence of a side door in the *skene* from which Clytaemestra now emerges, while the central door may now be thought of vaguely as the door inside the courtyard leading to the men's quarters. For the first time Clytaemestra is seen to be no longer in control of the central door. When she hears of Aegisthus' death, magnificent as ever in her defiance she calls for an axe with which to defend herself, but at this point the central door opens and it is Orestes who now stands there dominating the entrance. His mother bares her breast in an appeal for pity, and, although for the audience the appeal is somewhat weakened by its knowledge that Cilissa had been the real mother to the little boy, this is the most terrible moment in the play. For the first, and only, time Orestes weakens, as he utters the characteristic cry of the tragic hero, 'Pylades, what am I to do? Am I to feel shame at killing my mother?' For the first time he uses the word 'mother'. And now, at this crucial moment, Aeschylus surprises us again. Pylades, whom we had assumed to be a non-speaking extra (see p. 44), breaks his silence to remind Orestes of Apollo's oracle. Orestes' resolution is restored, and in a line-by-line stichomythia he has no difficulty in demolishing his mother's pleas for mercy and her warning of her avenging Erinyes. In *Agamemnon* the female Clytaemestra had defeated the male Agamemnon in a similar stichomythia (see p. 37). This time it is the male who wins. Clytaemestra at last understands the meaning of the snake in her dream. So she is led off to be killed beside her lover. The scene mirrors *Agamemnon*; in both plays we see a man and a woman passing through the central door to their deaths (see p. 39).

The Chorus sings a joyous and triumphant ode: justice has been done, the light can be seen again, and all the pollution will be driven from the house. The final scene begins on the same triumphant note. The central door opens, and reveals, probably on the *ekkyklema*, Orestes standing over the corpses of his two victims. Again the tableau mirrors *Agamemnon*, in which we saw Clytaemestra standing over the bodies of Agamemnon and Cassandra (see p. 40). Orestes orders the robe that enveloped Agamemnon in his bath to be unfolded before the eyes of the audience. He struggles to find the appropriate language to describe both his mother and the robe; she is best compared to a snake, and the robe to some kind of net. The mood of triumph, however, does not last. The Chorus is the first to introduce a sour note, as it laments the death even of Clytaemestra, and prophesies that 'suffering in fact bursts into flower for the one who is waiting'; in other words, it will soon be Orestes' turn to suffer' (cf. p. 47). Orestes tries to justify himself, but then feels madness coming upon him as he has a vision of his mother's avenging Furies, the snake-wreathed Erinyes. He who was warned by Apollo of his father's Erinyes should he fail to kill his mother is now to be pursued by his mother's Erinyes for carrying out the killing (cf. 924-5, p. 46). He refuses to accept the Chorus-leader's reassurance that they are all in his imagination. The play, which began with such high hopes for the young Orestes, ends with the realisation that pure motives are not enough. As in *Agamemnon* the initial hope has led only to disappointment. In this world it is the deed that counts.

It is a terrible crime to kill one's mother, and Orestes has the pollution of her blood on his hands. As he departs to seek the help of Apollo at Delphi, once more an exile from Argos, the Chorus can indulge only in the kind of wishful thinking that characterised *Agamemnon*: 'may you be happy, and may god graciously watch over you and guard you with timely fortunes'. In the closing anapaests it recalls the cannibal feast of Thyestes (see p. 39), and the murder of Agamemnon. This play has presented the 'third storm' in the house. It ought to be the last, but instead of salvation it has brought only doom. The final words of the play are 'where will it end? Where will the might of *Ate* (Ruin) go to sleep and stop?' There is no closure at all.

The Oresteia
(iii) Eumenides

Libation Bearers ended with the desperate appeal, 'where will it end?' In *Eumenides* the answer will be given at last with the acquittal of Orestes before the court of the Areopagus at Athens, and with the eventual agreement of the Erinyes, who form the Chorus of the play, to accept the verdict and, in their new identity as Eumenides, i.e. the 'Kindly Ones', to bless, instead of punish, Athens. The myth knew of no further manifestation of the curse on the house of Atreus beyond this point. In various versions Orestes was simply purified from his pollution in one place or another, while in the *Oresteia* of the early lyric poet Stesichorus, Apollo gave him a bow with which to defend himself against the Erinyes. In one version he was tried and acquitted before the twelve Olympian gods on the Areopagus. As far as we can tell, Aeschylus was the first to have him tried there in front of a human jury, and to link the story with the founding by Athena of the historical court of the Areopagus. Probably, but not certainly, he also introduced the identification of Erinyes and Eumenides, both chthonic groups of goddesses, but otherwise quite different in their nature. Perhaps the identification of the latter with the 'Awesome Goddesses', to whom there is an apparent reference at 1041, had already been made before Aeschylus. It is odd that the name Eumenides nowhere occurs in the play. It has been thought that it may have dropped out of our text after 1027 or 1028, or (Brown) that the identification is post-Aeschylean and that the original title of the play may have been 'Erinyes'.

The Areopagus, which consisted of ex-archons, had been entrusted by Solon with the guardianship of the Athenian laws. In 487 BC it had lost some of its powers when the lot was introduced for the appointment of archons, and in 462 BC the democrats enacted further reductions which left it with little more than jurisdiction in certain homicide trials. The matter was clearly topical in 458 BC, the year of the first production of *Eumenides*, and it is not surprising that scholars have tried to deduce Aeschylus' own political views from the play. Some have concluded that he was a political reactionary who wrote the play in protest against the recent reform, others that he was a moderate democrat who approved of it but aimed to warn his audience against any further changes, others again that nothing in the play prevents us from believing that he was a whole-hearted democrat. The wisest judgement is that Aeschylus carefully presented the matter in such a way as to avoid offending any section of his audience. Macleod argues that the Athens of *Eumenides* is to be seen, not in narrowly political terms, but as 'an ideal representation of human society which pointedly reverses the social disorder of the *Agamemnon* and *Choephori*' (p. 132). Nevertheless, in no other surviving play of Aeschylus, unless possibly *Suppliants*, does this kind of problem arise, and certainly not in the first two plays of the trilogy. Moreover, when three times in the play (289-91, 669-73, 762-4) it is stressed that Orestes' acquittal will lead to a permanent treaty between Athens and Argos, the original audience would think of the alliance agreed between these two cities at the end of the 460s. In this final play, then, the only extant tragedy to be set in the centre of Athens, Aeschylus' concerns evidently extend beyond the tragic history of the house of Atreus at Argos. Little more than two-thirds of the way through the play Orestes has departed from the stage, leaving the rest of it to deal with the reaction of the Erinyes and the foundation of their cult in a cave under the Acropolis.

Eumenides differs from *Agamemnon* and *Libation Bearers* also in that it is less concerned with the insoluble and universal problems of human motivation, responsibility, and guilt. The conflict is no longer so much between the Erinyes and Orestes as between the Erinyes and Apollo, Orestes' defender. In the first two plays the Olympian and chthonic deities were united, sharing the responsibility for every stage in the development of the curse. Apollo threatens Orestes with his father's Erinyes if he fails to kill his mother (see p. 46). Now, however, he has changed his position, and has become the opponent of the chthonic goddesses, whom he describes in the must unflattering of terms (185-97). When they claim (210-12, 604-5) to be concerned with murders only of blood-relations the Erinyes too have changed their standpoint. With his appointment of the Erinyes as Chorus, a group of goddesses who exist independently of the play, Aeschylus, as in *Suppliants* (see p. 26), experiments by giving his Chorus a principal role in the plot. We are as interested in what will happen to it as we are in the fate of Orestes. In *Suppliants*, however, the Danaids were *the* 'protagonist', whereas here the Erinyes share that role with the technical protagonist, Orestes. Related to all this is the fact that the language is on the whole more direct than in the first two plays. They were bound together by a complex of recurring images and themes. Some of them do appear from time to time in *Eumenides* (the idea that blood once shed can never be recalled at 261-3, 647-9, 479, the metaphor of hunting at 111-13, 131, 147-8, 231, 246-9), but they are generally less pervasive.

The play begins in front of the temple of Apollo at Delphi, to which we saw Orestes departing at the end of *Libation Bearers*. His pursuit by the Erinyes thus bridges the gap between the two plays. In the highly elaborate prologue the opening monologue resembles those of *Agamemnon* and *Libation Bearers*, especially the former in that it is delivered by a minor character who will not be seen again. All three begin with a prayer. Here it is to the various deities who have presided over, or been connected with, the sanctuary, the most recent of whom is Apollo. The peace and serenity of his temple contrast with the end of *Libation Bearers*, and prepare us for the resolution at the end of the play. In all three opening monologues something happens in the middle which gets the action underway. Here the Pythia, the Delphic priestess, having entered by a side-passage goes into the temple only to come rushing out immediately, probably on all fours, to report the shocking sight that has met her – Orestes at the navel-stone which marked the centre of the world, his hands dripping with blood, and near him the hideous Erinyes. In the first two plays the monologue comprised the whole of the prologue, but here much will happen as we are kept waiting for the *parodos* of the Chorus. First we see Apollo encouraging Orestes and sending him off, escorted by Hermes, on his long journey to Athens where he is to sit as a suppliant at Athena's statue, and where, Apollo promises him, he will be tried and released from his troubles (cf. the language of the opening line of *Agamemnon*). Next the ghost of Clytaemestra appears, the only character to figure in all three plays of the trilogy. In *Libation Bearers* she was frightened by her nightmare. Now it is her turn to appear in a dream, as she chides the sleeping Erinyes for showing ingratitude for all her offerings by neglecting their pursuit of Orestes. The Chorus gradually wakes up and prepares at last to sing the *parodos*.

No entirely satisfactory explanation has yet been given of how all this was staged. It is natural to suppose that the *skene* now serves as Apollo's temple, and that the Pythia enters it through the central door. But how, then, is the inside scene, from 64 to 179, made visible to the audience? – hardly through the open door, which at that time of year would have been in deep shadow for much of the day. Some theories involve the use of the *ekkyklema* (see p. 40), which, however, could not have been big enough to hold a chorus of twelve, together with Apollo, Orestes, and Hermes, to say nothing of the navel-stone. A possible compromise would involve the appearance of the *ekkyklema* at 64, carrying Orestes and two or three representative Erinyes, with Apollo and (if he appears at all) Hermes on the back of the platform; the rest of the Chorus would then begin to pour out of the door in time for the *parodos*. Taplin's view that the Chorus is not visible at all until the *parodos* is more consistent with normal tragic practice, and would make the sudden entry of the Erinyes all the more effective. Only Orestes and Apollo, then, would come out through the door at 64, but this scenario leads to problems when we consider the ghost-scene that begins at 94. It is hard to believe that Clytaemestra has come out on to the stage to appear in a dream to, and to rebuke, a Chorus which is still unseen inside the *skene*, and it would be only slightly better if she enters by a side-passage. We may reject the view that we only hear her voice from within the *skene*, and that the stage is completely empty from 94 to 142. For others the *skene* is not used at all; the stage-setting represents an *indoor* scene, and the Pythia enters the stage from the side, so that at first she does not see the Chorus which is already in position in the *orchestra*. Apart from the uncertainty as to whether the Greek stage and *orchestra* ever represent an indoor scene (see p. 11), this arrangement would surely weaken the effectiveness of the *parodos*.

The short *parodos*, in which the Chorus' entry, according to a late and unreliable source, caused children to faint and women to miscarry, establishes both the relentless determination of the Erinyes to pursue Orestes and their disapproval of Apollo, one (from their viewpoint) of the younger gods, for giving sanctuary to the impious man who murdered his mother. In *Agamemnon* we heard from Cassandra of a chorus of Erinyes singing its baleful hymn in Agamemnon's house. In *Libation Bearers* Orestes, but not the Chorus or the audience, saw them, wreathed in snakes, in his madness. Now we see them with our own eyes and hear their hymn. With the end of the ode, Apollo and the Chorus quarrel angrily. The latter makes it clear that Apollo is responsible for the whole situation (199-200). When asked by Apollo why the Erinyes did not pursue Clytaemestra for killing her husband, the Erinyes reply that their duty is to persecute only killers of kindred blood. This curious inconsistency with the first two plays of the trilogy (see p. 54 above) helps to prepare us for the argument in the trial-scene about the relationship between mother and son.

At 234 the Chorus resumes its pursuit of Orestes, and the stage and *orchestra* are left completely empty, a very rare occurrence in Greek tragedy. It is even rarer that when Orestes enters, closely followed by the Chorus, we are now in front of (some would say inside) Athena's temple on the Athenian Acropolis. The only parallel for such a change of scene is in Sophocles' *Ajax*, and even that is not accepted by everybody. Orestes claims that he is no longer polluted. When and where the purification took place is strangely unclear. According to 282-3 it was at Delphi (cf.

Libation Bearers 1059-60), but there was no mention of this in the prologue. Other passages (238-9, 451-2) suggest that it was long drawn out and in the course of his travels. Orestes' appeal to Athena to come and save him leaves the Chorus unimpressed, and it proceeds to sing a 'binding hymn', as it probably dances round its helpless victim who clings to Athena's statue, a song which combines chilling threats with what we may be surprised to find is a reasonable case for its own ancient allotted destiny as upholder of the social order. Athena arrives, and in a question-and-answer stichomythia listens to the Chorus' account of Orestes' crime. Unlike Apollo, Athena treats the Erinyes with courtesy. The Chorus with equal politeness agrees to accept her judgement in the matter. Then it is Orestes' turn in a long speech to plead his case; he is no longer polluted, and Apollo is responsible for Clytaemestra's death, having threatened him with terrible punishments if he should refuse to kill his mother. Athena resolves that the case is too serious for her to decide on her own; Orestes is her suppliant, but she recognises that the Erinyes if defeated are likely to take revenge on her city Athens. Her situation is not unlike that of Pelasgus in *Suppliants*. She goes off to choose the best Athenian citizens to form the jury of the court which she now proposes to institute, leaving the Chorus to lament the consequences for justice and morality if they are to be defeated, and if Orestes is to serve as a precedent for unpunished wrongdoing. It is unclear whether Orestes leaves too.

Athena returns to the stage with probably eleven (not ten or twelve; see below) jurors, and Apollo enters to defend Orestes. We seem now to be on the Areopagus below the Acropolis, but this time the change of scene, or rather refocusing, is hardly noticed. Scullion indeed thinks that we have not moved from Athena's temple at all. The voting urns are set out, and a trumpet is sounded to mark the beginning of the trial. Apollo begins by acknowledging his responsibility for the matricide. The Chorus-leader interrogates Orestes in stichomythia, in the course of which Orestes asks, as Apollo did earlier (see p. 56), why the Erinyes did not pursue Clytaemestra for her husband's murder. Again the answer is that husband and wife are not blood relations. Apollo now takes over from Orestes, who will not speak again until 746 when the votes have been cast. Apollo claims to be the spokesman of Zeus himself, and goes on to argue that the murder of the woman Clytaemestra was a much less serious matter than the killing by a woman of a noble man, a king who had returned successfully from war. Apollo's male chauvinism may have offended a fifth-century audience less than a modern one. But any audience would notice the weakness of Apollo's position when he is trapped into proclaiming one of the recurring ideas of the trilogy, that blood once shed can never be recalled. 'Exactly', cries the Chorus-leader, 'so how can you defend Orestes for spilling his mother's blood?' This leads to the notorious speech in which Apollo argues that the mother is not really a parent of the child but merely the repository of her husband's seed, as Athena herself would testify, having been born from the head of Zeus, without the need for a mother. We cannot tell whether this argument would seem as ludicrous to an ancient as to a modern audience. There is indeed evidence that the view was held by certain, but by no means all, scientists and medical writers at the time. The relationship between the sexes has been an important theme from the beginning of the trilogy, and the status of motherhood was an issue in *Libation Bearers*, where the biological mother Clytaemestra was less of a real mother than the nurse Cilissa. Now we learn that the mother is not a biological parent at all. It is slightly disappointing that the theme has been reduced to an intellectual and sophistic argument. Is it really more acceptable for a man to kill his mother than for a wife to murder her husband? Finally Apollo resorts to bribery; if the jury acquits Orestes, he and his descendants will be the allies of Athens for evermore (see p. 54).

Athena declares that enough has been said and that it is time for the jury to vote, but first she pronounces the charter of the new court. When she encourages the people to respect neither anarchy nor despotism (696-7), it is significant that her language recalls that of the Chorus itself at 526-30. When too she declares that there is a place for fear in a well-governed city her position is again not so far removed from that of the Erinyes. At last the jurors take it in turn to drop their votes into the urns. Athena is the last to vote. She says that she will vote in Orestes' favour; not having a mother herself, she naturally prefers the man. Finally she declares that if the votes turn out to be equal that will mean acquittal. Since they are, in fact, equal, Orestes is duly acquitted.

There has been much debate as to how all this was arranged. It may seem an unimportant detail, but in fact it will affect our understanding of the resolution at the end of the play. Most modern scholars believe that the human jurors were equally divided, and that Athena's vote is simply the casting vote that equal votes should count as acquittal. The structure of the scene, however, and the language suggest that the other view is correct, that the majority of the human jurors actually vote for condemnation, and that it is Athena's vote that produces the equality, which at the second stage is declared to mean acquittal. From 711-33 the Chorus and Apollo deliver eleven alternate couplets (except that the final one is a triplet), during or after each of which presumably one of eleven jurors casts his vote. Athena then places her vote in the urn, as she declares her preference for the male, the head of the household. Only then does she explain what will happen if the votes are now equal. She does *not* say that a vote from her will be required *only* if the human jurors fail to agree.

The scene concludes rapidly with a grateful and joyous speech from Orestes, thanking Athena, Apollo, and Zeus the Third the Saviour, no longer in a blasphemous context as at *Agamemnon* 1387 (see p. 40), and confirming the future alliance between Argos and Athens. Orestes departs, and we shall not see him again. So does Apollo, who does not speak at all. The audience doubtless noticed his departure, but so unobtrusive is it that modern scholars argue about when it actually takes place.

Contrast the departure of the Chorus, which will not take place until the end of the play, nearly 300 lines later. From now on we almost forget Orestes, as our attention is turned to the reaction of the Erinyes, and to the, ultimately successful, attempt of Athena to pacify them and to persuade them not to send plagues on Athens but to bless the city instead. At last in this trilogy persuasion is used for a healthy purpose. Athena begins by arguing that, since the votes were equal, they have not really been defeated, and she tries to bribe them by offering them a sanctuary beneath the earth (i.e. in a cave near the Areopagus), in which they will receive a cult. At first she makes no impression. The Chorus repeats in lyric verse a chilling stanza, first heard before Athena's speech. Next she tries threats; she knows where the key is kept to the room where Zeus stores his thunderbolt. Athena remains polite and courteous throughout. Eventually the Chorus-leader takes over from the Chorus, and in less excited dialogue metre begins to show an interest in the new home that Athena is offering, and it is soon accepted. The Chorus sings a hymn for blessings on Athens, with interlocking anapaestic contributions from Athena. In its comprehensiveness it is comparable with the Danaids' prayer for blessings on Argos in *Suppliants* (see p. 30), and it contrasts effectively with all the curses earlier in the play. As it comes to an end, a secondary chorus of Athenians (probably Athena's female temple-servants, but some suppose that they are the members of the jury) enters to escort the Chorus to its new home. Before they all leave, the Erinyes, now Eumenides, put on crimson robes over their black garments as a token of their new status. Crimson, or dark red, was the colour of the fabrics over which Agamemnon walked into the house to his doom, and of the robe that trapped him in his bath. At last it connotes not bloodshed but something joyful and healthy. At last too, with the establishment of the new cult of the Eumenides, the perversion of sacrifice and religious ritual in the service of murder has been removed. The procession as it leaves the *orchestra* carries torches, a light that at last will not be turned into darkness. For the audience it probably resembled its beloved Panathenaic procession.

So impressive and spectacular is the ending of the play that the audience is doubtless meant to feel that the problems of the trilogy have been solved, that closure has been achieved. Yet for some at least of the spectators a few niggling doubts may remain. There is no space here to discuss the question of whether a play that ends happily can be a tragedy, or, in this case, whether a trilogy that ends happily can be described as tragic because its first two plays undoubtedly deserve that description. And, if Aeschylus seriously wants us to believe that good government in a city, even an ideal city rather than the real democracy of Athens in 458 BC, is, like good behaviour in an individual, a guarantee of prosperity and success, we may want to disagree (see p. 10). But what exactly is the nature of the resolution? We can hardly say that light as represented by Apollo has triumphed over darkness in the form of the Erinyes. Although Winnington-Ingram perhaps exaggerates the discreditable flaws in Apollo's position in the trilogy, it is true that his role, especially in the trial-scene, is remarkably unimpressive. In many respects, as we have seen, Athena seems to be more closely affiliated to the Erinyes, who have made out a good case for themselves as upholders of morality. Nor are they really converted into goddesses of a different kind. Athena herself confirms them in their ancient role of pursuing inherited guilt (932-7; cf. 954-5). They are still chthonic deities, and as such they have the power both to harm and to bless. What does appear to be new is that a way has been found for replacing the blood-feud with an objective trial in a court of law. Retribution need no longer incur further guilt. So Orestes is acquitted, but only through what may seem to be an arbitrary decision by Athena, which on this occasion the Erinyes are persuaded to accept. With the most probable view of the voting (see pp. 58-9) the human jurors judged him to be guilty, and, even if the other view is favoured, they were equally divided. It is difficult to see how Aeschylus could have made it clearer that the problems of the first two plays are insoluble, at least on the human level. *Was* Orestes right to kill his mother?

Prometheus Bound

The play presents the story of the punishment of the pre-Olympian god Prometheus for stealing fire from the gods and giving it to human beings. Altogether four *Prometheus* plays were attributed to Aeschylus in antiquity. *Prometheus Pyrkaeus* was almost certainly the satyr-play presented along with *Persians*, while *Prometheus Pyrphoros* (*Fire-Bearer*) and *Prometheus Lyomenos* (*Unbound*) have generally, but not always, been assumed to be associated with *Prometheus Desmotes* (*Bound*) as comprising a connected trilogy (from time to time a dilogy of *Bound* and *Unbound* has been suggested. Brown argues that *Pyrkaeus* and *Pyrphoros* are the same play). If this is correct, *Pyrphoros* is likely to have preceded *Bound*, and to have dealt with Prometheus' theft of fire from the gods, or, less likely, may have come third, with its theme derived perhaps from the *Promethia*, the Athenian torch-festival of the god.

There is no indication that the authenticity of any of these plays was ever suspected in antiquity. It was not until the nineteenth century that doubts began to be expressed. They resurfaced in the first decades of the twentieth century, but it was only with the publication of Mark Griffith's book in 1977 that, although some influential voices still maintain the authenticity of the play, majority opinion may be said to have turned against it. One problem has been to reconcile the picture of Zeus in *Bound* as a cruel tyrant with the other six surviving plays, but that in itself is not conclusive; in *Unbound*, he may have been presented very differently. In our play there is much stress on the fact that Zeus is a young god who has only recently come to power (for the tension between new and an earlier generation of gods compare *Eumenides*), and many have supposed that we are to think of an evolving Zeus (some have found the same notion in the *Oresteia*).

More serious are considerations of structure and style. Every other one of the other plays can be shown to differ from the rest in one respect or another, but *Bound* stands alone in differing from all the others in *most* of the features of language and style that can be isolated or counted, not least in the relative simplicity of its imagery and in its treatment of the choral odes and their metres. When before the *parodos* Prometheus at last gives tongue to lament his misfortunes, he employs a mixture of dialogue iambic metre and sung lyric, while Io sings a monody at 566-608. In none of the other six plays does an actor ever sing unless it is as part of an *epirrhematikon*. Many of the individual differences can be explained away, but cumulatively the evidence is overwhelming. Attempts to account for them in terms of the supposed date of the play are unconvincing – whether early (for in some respects our play seems close to Sophocles, and to betray an interest in sophistic ideas which suggests a date of composition in the 440s or 430s), or late (for Aeschylus' death only two years after his production of the *Oresteia* leaves no room for such a radical development). Nor is there any obvious reason why, if he wrote the play in Sicily, he should have wanted to change so radically the way in which he composed. It has been suggested that Aeschylus left the play unrevised at the time of his death, and that it was produced posthumously by, for example, his son Euphorion. If so, he must have been intending to revise almost everything in it. More plausible is the view of West that Euphorion, who is known to have been himself a playwright, could have written the trilogy and attributed it to his father.

The structure of the play is very simple. It begins with the nailing of Prometheus to his rock in the wilds of uninhabited Scythia, and it ends with his being cast down by Zeus into Tartarus in an earthquake and whirlwind. When he is eventually restored to the light the eagle, the bird of Zeus, will come every day to feast on his liver. From beginning to end Prometheus remains immobile on the stage, providing the drama with its most obvious unity. Probably no one now believes that the actor spoke his lines unseen from behind or inside a giant dummy representing Prometheus, but it is certainly true that the role must have been a particularly arduous one for the actor. Aristotle in his *Poetics* distinguished 'simple' from 'complex' plots, in that they did not contain a 'reversal' or a 'recognition'. By this token most of Aeschylus' surviving plays might be said to have 'simple' plots, But *Prometheus* would seem to answer to Aristotle's definition of the extreme type of 'simple' plot, the 'episodic', the kind that Aristotle liked least. There is little real sense of a carefully constructed dramatic unity, in which each scene develops out of the preceding scene(s) in a logical and coherent manner. Instead, we have a series of self-contained scenes in which the immobile Prometheus receives a series of visitors in no very obvious order. Why does the playwright choose Oceanus in particular, when he has no obvious connection with the Prometheus story? We have to work it out for ourselves that he is the father-in-law of Prometheus, and the fact that the members of the Chorus are Io's aunts is mentioned only at 636. The relationship between Oceanus and the Chorus, his daughters, is dramatically of no importance, but it is still odd that neither even acknowledges the on-stage presence of the other. Io is not normally connected with Prometheus, but her presence in the play is justified by the fact that she too is a victim of Zeus who will one day be delivered from her troubles, and that she will turn out to be the ancestress of Prometheus' eventual deliverer. Moreover, her agitated movements and frenzied wanderings will contrast effectively with the immobility of Prometheus.

There is some point to the arrangement. In terms of the relationship between Prometheus and his various visitors each scene provides some kind of contrast with the preceding scene. The prologue presents one god, Hephaestus, who is sympathetic to Prometheus, and one, Power, who, as the servant of Zeus, is one of his enemies. Thereafter friends and enemies alternate. Enter the Chorus of daughters of Oceanus, who are entirely sympathetic to the hero and whose visit Prometheus welcomes. Next we meet Oceanus himself, whose sympathy seems to Prometheus to be skin-deep, and whose attempt at comfort he rejects. Oceanus is only too happy to depart from the scene so as to avoid trouble for himself. With cow-horned Io we return to someone with whom Prometheus can identify as a fellow-victim of Zeus. In *Suppliants* the same Io served at every point as a parallel for the suffering of the Danaid chorus. Perhaps this gave the author of *Prometheus* the cue for turning her into an actual character on the stage. Next we encounter Hermes, another lackey of Zeus, and another enemy, whose threats rouse Prometheus into displaying the full strength of his hatred and his determination. Finally we return to the relationship between Prometheus and the Chorus, his sympathisers throughout the play. In contrast to the timidity which they have previously shown, they now surprise us by declaring their resolve to stay beside Prometheus, and despite the threats of Hermes they duly descend with the hero into Tartarus, the only visitors to remain with him till the end. The play began with the juxtaposition of the cruel Power and the sympathetic Hephaestus. It ends with that of Hermes and the Chorus.

The principal unifying factor in the drama is the secret which Prometheus holds concerning the future fate of Zeus himself. According to the myth, Zeus learned from Themis that Thetis was fated to bear a son who would be more powerful than his father. He therefore changed his mind about marrying her, and instead gave her as wife to the mortal Peleus, and Achilles was their son. In our play Themis has revealed the secret to her son Prometheus, whose possession of it 'becomes the key to the resolution of the whole drama' (Griffith, edn 6). When the Chorus at 165-7 first introduces the possibility that someone may one day supplant

Zeus Prometheus forecasts that the time will indeed come when Zeus will need him, because he has a secret that he will refuse to divulge until Zeus sets him free and offers appropriate compensation. As the play progresses it becomes increasingly clear that the liberation of Prometheus depends entirely on Zeus changing his mind (257-8, 375-6), but that it is as yet too early for Prometheus to use his secret. In Homer the relationship between Zeus and Fate is left uncertain. At 511-20 Prometheus declares that Zeus is weaker than Fate.

As Prometheus gradually reveals more, but not all, of his secret, inconsistencies begin to appear in his prophecies. He tells us that Zeus will enter into a marriage which he will regret (764, 907-10), and that he, Prometheus, will be released from his troubles by one of Io's descendants, Heracles (772-4, 871-3). The order of events is far from clear. Will Zeus release Prometheus in order to persuade him to divulge his secret (so e.g. 989-91), or will he set him free in gratitude for having done so? It is odd too that he states so categorically, especially in the final scene, that Zeus *will* be removed from his throne, when the audience must know that there will in fact be a reconciliation. A further complication is introduced when Hermes declares that Prometheus' troubles will continue until one of the gods agrees to take his place in Tartarus (1026-9). He means 'never', but the audience will remember that in some versions of the story the Centaur Chiron or Heracles actually did this. It may be that the knowledge of Prometheus himself is limited (so Bollack). But we should notice also how he grows in confidence and determination as the play progresses. As Sommerstein puts it, his silence at the beginning marked his powerlessness, whereas his silence at the end concerning his secret is a mark of his power; 'it is that movement in the balance of power that constitutes the real action of *Prometheus Bound*' (*Aeschylean Tragedy* 309). Throughout all this the playwright keeps his audience in suspense by suggesting various possible ways in which the plot of the following play may develop. The technique is certainly not unknown to Aeschylus, but here it is perhaps less skilfully handled.

The same can be said of other elements of plot-construction. At 282 the Chorus is ready to hear about the future troubles of Prometheus when the sudden arrival of Oceanus intervenes, and it will be nearly 500 lines before Prometheus is able to satisfy its wish. At 630-1 Prometheus is about to respond to Io's request for information about *her* future troubles, when the Chorus-leader asks that Io may first describe those which she has already suffered. Attention is drawn to this arrangement after Io has made her speech. At 778 Prometheus offers Io a choice: he will either tell her of what lies ahead for her or he will reveal the identity of the one who will set him free; for some reason he does not wish to do both. The Chorus-leader, however, is inclined to bargain, and persuades Prometheus both to favour the Chorus by revealing his future saviour, and to gratify Io's request for information about what is to happen to her; cf. also 819-22. It is hard to see the point of all this. It seems so much less serious than the suspense of the audience of, for example, *Libation Bearers* when it waits to see whether Aegisthus or Clytaemestra will come out of the palace-door.

There can be little doubt that in this quarrel between Prometheus and Zeus the audience is meant from the beginning of the play to take the side of the former (for a different view, that the plan of Zeus for mortals is essentially benign, and that Prometheus deserves his punishment, see White). Both Power and Hephaestus make it clear already in the prologue that Prometheus is being punished not only for his theft of fire but for his *philanthropos* (human-loving) character in general (11, 28). The same reason for Zeus' hatred is given by Prometheus himself (119-23). Conversely Zeus had planned to destroy the whole human race and to replace it with another, and was prevented from doing so only by Prometheus (232-4). The only human character in the play is Io, and she too is one of his victims. In his speeches to the Chorus at 436-71 and 476-506 Prometheus can claim not only to have given human beings fire but to have bestowed on them all the arts and skills and all the benefits of civilised life: 'all skills have come to mortals from Prometheus' (506). It is equally clear from the prologue onwards that Zeus is to be regarded as a harsh and despotic tyrant. Even his servant Power can say 'no one is free except for Zeus' (50). The words 'tyrant' and 'tyranny', which are frequently used of him, in tragedy may sometimes be applied neutrally to any king, good or bad, but the context, as here, often makes it clear that they carry a derogatory sense. The unpleasant Power at the beginning and Hermes at the end leave us in no doubt about the unpleasantness of the master whom they represent. Moreover, as Prometheus complains (975-6, 985) he has shown gross ingratitude to Prometheus to whom he owed his victory in the struggle with the Titans (197-241, 439-40).

In many ways Prometheus may be compared with the Sophoclean hero, who remains true to himself and who refuses to accept the advice of ordinary, lesser characters that he should learn sense or compromise or yield or be persuaded. 'Know yourself and adapt new ways', says Oceanus (309-10), and 'you are not yet humble, nor do you submit (*eikeis*, a key Sophoclean word) to your misfortunes' (320). Even Hermes, having complained that he has not yet learnt good sense (*sophrosyne* 982), tries to 'persuade' him with his words (1014) to give up his stubbornness and divulge his secret. His words are really threats, but the Chorus too urges him to be persuaded (1037-9). We admire Prometheus, and it is not surprising that he has so often been seen, especially in the Romantic period, as a prototype of all rebels against authority. From time to time, however, the playwright raises, without ever fully developing, the question of Prometheus' responsibility for his own suffering. When Power uses the word *hamartia* to describe the actions for which he must be punished (9), he certainly means it in its moral sense of 'wrongdoing', as does Hermes when he employs the verb *(ex)hamartano* at 945, but what does the Chorus mean at 260 and 1039 – perhaps 'make a mistake'? Strangest of all is the apparent confession of Prometheus himself at 266: 'I committed *hamartia* voluntarily, voluntarily [i.e. in helping mortals]; I shall not deny it.' Are we to suppose that the use of the verb is sarcastic, or that he is merely acknowledging that in helping human beings he made a mistake in that he was acting against his own interests? There are similar ambiguities in the use of *amplakema* and *amplakia* at 112, 386, 563, and 620. The Chorus is critical too of Prometheus' stubbornness and excessive freedom of speech at 178-80 (cf. 472-5). The audience may well feel that it cannot have been morally wrong for Prometheus to love the human race, but that it is an error of judgement for him to refuse to divulge his secret to Zeus. We admire him, but we would find it difficult to be like him. In the final lines of the play even Prometheus confesses that he is afraid (1090; cf. 127).

The staging of *Prometheus* presents insoluble problems. Scholars are divided as to whether the rock is represented by, or is a construction set against, the *skene* at the back of the *orchestra*, or whether it is in the middle of the *orchestra*. The Chorus has flown across the sky from home on a winged car. In the post-Aeschylean theatre the *mechane* (crane) might be used to bring on a god by swinging him or her over the roof of the *skene*. It was not employed by Aeschylus in any of the six surviving plays. Even if it was available to the writer of this play, a crane which could carry a chorus of twelve or fifteen, and on which it remained for 150 lines, is scarcely credible. West's theory that there were several, perhaps six, cranes projecting above the tops of two wooden screens, is too elaborate to carry conviction. Some scholars suppose that the Chorus enters the *orchestra*, or appears on the *skene* roof, in one or more wheeled vehicles. This last solution would have the advantage of explaining the failure of Oceanus and the Chorus to make any contact with each other; during the Oceanus-scene the Chorus is on its way down behind the *skene*. If, however, Prometheus is positioned in front of the *skene*, he would be unable to see the Chorus on the roof. Another view is that the Chorus simply dances into the *orchestra*, via a side-passage, having left its car off stage, but it is then hard to explain Prometheus' instruction to it to come down on to the ground at 272, or the Chorus' description of its descent at 278-80. The entrance of Oceanus himself on his fantastic winged griffin would certainly be achieved most easily by means of the *mechane*, if it existed at this time, bearing some kind of stage-bird on which Oceanus sits. His comical excuse for his hasty departure is that the griffin is giving signs that it is eager to get home (394-6).

Most difficult of all is the staging of the cataclysm with which the play ends, as Prometheus and the Chorus are cast down into Tartarus. Some believe that they disappear through the door of the *skene*, perhaps on the *ekkyklema*, a manoeuvre that was probably beyond the resources of the fifth-century theatre, and leaves unexplained how Prometheus gets on to the *ekkyklema* if he is still chained to his rock. A compromise theory is that only Prometheus is swallowed up by the central door, while the Chorus runs away in terror, thereby ruining the effect of its declaration of solidarity. For others, the whole thing is left entirely, or mainly, to the imagination of the audience, guided by the words and the movements of the Chorus. If Prometheus' position is in the centre of the *orchestra*, it is difficult to see how else it could be done. The play, then, comes to an end (in the modern theatre the curtain would fall), and actor and Chorus simply walk out of the *orchestra*, in what would surely be a disappointing anticlimax.

Epilogue

In the *Oresteia* trilogy, as we have seen, all three plays are connected in their subject-matter, as they present successive episodes in the story of the house of Atreus, with the lost satyr-play which followed the tragedies also drawn from the same myth. This was almost certainly true also of the trilogies to which *Seven against Thebes* and *Suppliants* belonged. We do not know whether Aeschylus was the first, or the only tragedian of his time, to organise his plays in this way. *Persians*, however, although it may have had some thematic links with the tragedies that preceded and followed it, was certainly not part of a connected trilogy in the same sense. From what is known about the lost plays one may deduce that Aeschylus often, but not invariably, did present connected trilogies. But we cannot assume that they were all as closely connected as the plays of the *Oresteia* trilogy. Too many have attempted to reconstruct the missing plays on the basis of a single surviving instance, and on the assumption that we are familiar with Aeschylus' *normal* practice in constructing his trilogies. Sophocles evidently gave up the practice, preferring to present unconnected tragedies. This Epilogue will take no account of the un-Aeschylean *Prometheus*.

Despite the danger of generalising about the Aeschylean trilogy, it is not unreasonable to suppose that he chose it because it enabled him to present a tragedy that was wider than that of an individual sufferer – one that carried on over several generations of a family. This may take the form of an inherited curse, or inherited guilt, which, as West points out, is not necessarily the same thing. In the *Oresteia* Thyestes' curse on Atreus passes on to Agamemnon and then to Orestes. In the trilogy to which *Seven against Thebes* belonged, however, while Eteocles and Polyneices were certainly cursed by Oedipus, it is by no means certain that, in Aeschylus' version, there was any curse on Laius in the previous generation (see p. 17). In *Suppliants* there is no family-curse, but at every stage the Danaids see themselves as re-enacting the story of their ancestress Io. The idea of the family-curse or inherited guilt is related to the belief that the children may have to pay for the sins of the fathers, which is a useful way of accounting both for crimes which apparently go unpunished by the gods and for suffering which is apparently undeserved. In Aeschylus, however, the question of responsibility is never as simple as that. In *Agamemnon* there is no mention of the family-curse until the Cassandra scene, late in the play. The starting-point of the tragedy is the departure of the expedition for Troy, as commanded by Zeus himself, and the decision taken by Agamemnon to sacrifice his daughter, the decision for which he is condemned by the Chorus. Other offences of Agamemnon follow. He deserves to die, but Clytaemestra's murder of her husband is a crime, so that she too deserves her death, but matricide is a further crime for which Orestes is rightly pursued by the Erinyes. Both Apollo and the underworld powers demand that he kill his mother, but at the same time we see him taking the responsibility upon himself. In the case of Eteocles the same sense of dual responsibility dominates the great central scene.

No major character in Aeschylus suffers simply because he is cursed, or somehow fated to do so. What is inherited is not only the curse or the guilt but the propensity to incur fresh guilt. Nor does anyone suffer without being under some kind of constraint to act as he does. It may seem illogical, but it is not untrue to human experience. The decisions that we make are not made in a vacuum; they are determined in varying degrees by circumstances which are often beyond our control. Sometimes, through no fault of our own we may be put in a situation where we are forced to make a decision between two courses of action both of which seem wrong. But we are still responsible for the decision that we make.

In *Eumenides* a way is found of bringing to an end the apparently endless chain of crime and retribution, and yet the sense of closure is not entirely complete. The Danaid trilogy may have presented some kind of resolution at the end. But we should not take it for granted that this was Aeschylus' normal practice. *Seven against Thebes* presents no resolution, unless it consists in the wiping out of the royal line. Alternatively we look ahead at the end to the continuation of the family's troubles (see p. 24). Even in *Persians*, which is not part of a connected trilogy, the foreboding continues beyond the end of the play, as we look forward to Plataea. In the *Oresteia*, particularly in the first two plays, this sense of an endless chain of crime and punishment, cause and effect, is strengthened in remarkable fashion by a complex system of interlocking metaphors and recurring ideas which connect up all the situations of the plays. Often the language of the metaphors glides imperceptibly between the tenor (the literal idea) and the vehicle (the figurative idea), and often what is figurative at one stage of the drama is realised literally at another. The symbolism of light and darkness is made visible to the Watchman at the beginning of *Agamemnon*, and almost visible to the audience through

Clytaemestra's beacon speech. In *Libation Bearers* darkness shrouds the house, while Electra longs for the return of Orestes to be the light of the house. It is not until the torchlight procession that brings the trilogy to an end that the darkness is finally conquered. In her vision Cassandra sees Clytaemestra as a snake, as does Orestes in *Libation Bearers*. But Orestes is the snake in his mother's dream, and in *Eumenides* the audience sees the snake-wreathed Erinyes. The idea that blood once shed can never be recalled reverberates throughout the trilogy, connecting up all the episodes in an unbreakable chain of cause and effect. Every time that we hear someone say 'let us hope that it may all turn out well', we shudder because we know that it never does.

In Aeschylus' other extant plays the imagery is on the whole simpler, but in all of them there are recurring metaphors and ideas. In *Seven against Thebes* the dominant metaphor is that of the ship of state, and it has been shown by Thalmann that the development of this and other nautical imagery reflects the dramatic shift in interest from the city to the family in the course of the play. We have no means of telling whether it ran through the whole trilogy. As an isolated play there was less scope for the technique in *Persians*, but the recurring metaphor of the yoke is handled most effectively. To impose a yoke of slavery on Greece Xerxes yokes the Hellespont, but in her dream Atossa sees her son's chariot crash with its yoke broken. The young Persian wives, newly yoked in marriage, having now lost their husbands, have become 'yoked all alone', and Xerxes finds that the yoke that he had imposed on his existing subjects, is now unloosed. The theme of the huge number of the Persian forces, which is so strongly stressed at the beginning of the play, turns into that of the huge number of the dead, now that Persia has been emptied of its men. Already in *Persians* the symbolism of light and darkness plays an important part. In general Aeschylus' language can be difficult. A tremendous amount of meaning may be packed into a single complex phrase. He is a prodigious creator of compound adjectives, which he likes to string together, with each bringing out a different aspect of the noun which they qualify, and with little concern for the precise logical connection between them; what matters is the total effect. Often the language seems to be deliberately ambiguous. On the other hand Aeschylus can write very simply and clearly when it suits his purpose.

Aeschylus is credited with the introduction of a second actor to a genre that had till then been performed entirely by a single actor and a chorus. We can only speculate about the difference that this must have made, but it is likely to have marked a major advance in the development of drama. Towards the end of his life he adopted Sophocles' introduction of a third actor. Since, however, the six surviving plays of Aeschylus all belong to a period of only fourteen years in his life, we cannot follow his development from youthful work to his ripe maturity. Among the six there are differences that are not to be explained in terms of the date of their production. In *Suppliants*, and to a lesser extent in *Eumenides*, Aeschylus experiments by assigning the principal dramatic role not to the technical protagonist, i.e. the first actor, but to the Chorus. The subject of *Persians* is drawn from recent history, instead of from the mythological world. In *Persians* and *Suppliants* for dramatic reasons he begins the plays with the *parodos* of the Chorus, instead of with a spoken prologue. Even within the trilogy there are differences between the first two plays and the third. By line 257 of *Agamemnon* we have arrived only at the end of the *parodos*, whereas at that point in *Eumenides*, we have already had a highly elaborate prologue containing a series of rapid scenes, and the setting of the play has changed from Delphi to Athens.

Nevertheless, it is possible to make some reasonably safe generalisations about the construction of Aeschylus' plays. Aristotle in his *Poetics* (see p. 62) distinguishes between what he calls complex and simple plots. He does not name Aeschylus in this context, but it is reasonable to suppose that for Aristotle Aeschylus in general wrote plays with 'simple' plots. There is for Agamemnon a reversal and a discovery of a kind, but they do not provide the basic structure of the whole play, as they do in *Oedipus the King*. Rather, Aeschylus' plays proceed in a more or less straight line from initial anxiety and foreboding to the fulfilment of our fears. In Sophocles the audience knows more than the unsuspecting characters, whereas in Aeschylus the audience shares the anxiety which is expressed by at least some of the characters from the beginning.

Yet the line of development is never completely straight. Aeschylus still manages to surprise us by manipulating our expectation of what is going to happen. In *Persians* the Chorus early in the play advises the anxious Atossa to make offerings to the underworld powers. Later we see her leaving the stage to make the appropriate arrangements. The long-awaited arrival of Xerxes seems to be imminent. We are therefore surprised to learn that the offerings are to be used to summon from the underworld the ghost of Darius, who will make his spectacular appearance before we are finally allowed to see Xerxes in his rags. In *Seven against Thebes* everyone in the audience knows that Eteocles and Polyneices will kill each other in single combat, but during the long central scene with its seven pairs of speeches, as we identify with the characters, we find ourselves irrationally hoping that somehow the tragedy may be averted. In *Suppliants*, after the Danaids have been granted asylum and while they sing their song of blessings on Argos we almost forget that they are still in danger from their cousins, so that the arrival of the Herald comes as an unpleasant shock. In *Libation Bearers* Aeschylus keeps us in suspense as to whether it is Aegisthus or Clytaemestra who will appear at the great door of the palace. It turns out to be Clytaemestra, and for a moment we expect Orestes to kill his mother immediately. Instead we have the courteous offer and acceptance of hospitality between Clytaemestra and Orestes, which makes us almost, but not quite, forget that the guest is about to kill his hostess. Regularly Aeschylus almost teases us when he ends a scene by hinting at what is going to happen in the next scene, before turning our minds away from it in an intervening choral ode. In *Agamemnon* he draws attention to the presence of Cassandra in Agamemnon's chariot, but we are kept waiting to find out what her dramatic role is to be. First the Chorus sings an anxious ode, at the end of which we expect to hear the death-cries of Agamemnon, or to see a messenger emerging from the palace with the news of the king's death. Instead, it is Clytaemestra who comes out through the door, and it is the Cassandra-scene that follows.

We are told by several ancient sources that Aeschylus' plays were so popular that after his death permission was, unusually, given for them to be reproduced, and that some of them won posthumous prizes in the dramatic competition. We know little about the work of his contemporary playwrights, but we may feel confident that the authorities in selecting him for this honour made the right decision.

Suggestions for Further Reading

Texts, Commentaries and Translations
All the plays may be found in two volumes in the Loeb Classical Library, edited, with introduction, Greek text, and English translation, and with fuller notes than is usual with this series, by A.H. Sommerstein (2008; vol. 3 contains the fragments); and in Oxford World's Classics, translated, and with extensive notes, by C. Collard, *Aeschylus Oresteia* (2002), *Aeschylus Persians and Other Plays* (2008). The following individual plays appear in the Aris & Phillips series (Warminster), with introduction, Greek text and English translation, and with a commentary based on the translation: *Persians*, E. Hall (1996); *Prometheus Bound*, A.J. Podlecki (2005); *Eumenides*, A.J. Podlecki (1989). In Greek Tragedy in New Translations: *The Complete Aeschylus*, 2 vols, ed. P. Burian and A. Shapiro (Oxford 2003 and 2009), the *Oresteia* (vol. 1) is translated by Shapiro and Burian, *Persians* by J. Lembke and C.J. Herington, *Seven against Thebes* by A. Hecht and H. Bacon, *Suppliants* by J. Lembke, and *Prometheus Bound* by J. Scully and C.J. Herington. Other translations are of *Seven against Thebes* by C.M. Dawson (Englewood Cliffs 1970); of *Suppliants* by P. Burian (Princeton 1991); and by P. Sandin, with introduction, Greek text, and commentary, but only of lines 1-523 (corrected edn Lund 2005); of the *Oresteia*, 3 vols, by H. Lloyd-Jones (Englewood Cliffs 1970; 2nd edn London 1979); and by R. Fagles (Penguin 1966). In the Everyman translations of the *Oresteia* (1995) and the other plays (1996) by M. Ewans the commentaries deal mainly, but not exclusively, with matters of performance. The following editions in the Cambridge Greek and Latin Classics series are intended primarily for readers who know Greek, but at least their introductions are generally accessible to Greekless readers: *Prometheus Bound*, M. Griffith (1983), *Eumenides*, A.H. Sommerstein (1989). J.C. Hogan's *Commentary on the Complete Greek Tragedies: Aeschylus* (Chicago and London 1984) is based on the Chicago translations edited by D. Grene and R. Lattimore.

Books
The following list is highly selective, and is restricted to those titles for which a knowledge of the language is not essential, most or all of the Greek being translated into English.

(a) General
Easterling, P.E. (ed.), *The Cambridge Companion to Greek Tragedy* (Cambridge 1997).
Heath, M., *The Poetics of Greek Tragedy* (London 1987).
Kitto, H.D.F., *Form and Meaning in Drama: a Study of Six Greek Plays and of* Hamlet (London 1956): especially for the *Oresteia*.
Rehm, R., *Greek Tragic Theatre* (London 1992).
Taplin, O., *Greek Tragedy in Action* (London 1978): especially for the *Oresteia*.

(b) Aeschylus
Conacher, D.J., *Aeschylus' Prometheus Bound: a Literary Commentary* (Toronto 1980).
——— *Aeschylus' Oresteia: a Literary Commentary* (Toronto 1987).
——— *Aeschylus: the Earlier Plays and Related Studies* (Toronto 1996).
Gagarin, M., *Aeschylean Drama* (California 1976).
Goldhill, S., *Aeschylus: the Oresteia* (Cambridge 1992).
Goward, B., *Aeschylus: Agamemnon* (Duckworth Companions to Greek and Roman Tragedy, London 2005).
Hall, E., *Inventing the Barbarian: Greek Self-definition through Tragedy* (Oxford 1989): especially for *Persians*.
Harrison, T., *The Emptiness of Asia: Aeschylus' Persians and the History of the Fifth Century* (Oxford 2000).
Herington, C.J., *Aeschylus* (New Haven and London 1986).
Ireland, S., *Aeschylus* (*Greece & Rome* New Surveys in the Classics 10, 1986).
Lebeck, A., *The Oresteia: a Study in Language and Structure* (Washington 1971).
Lloyd, M., *Oxford Readings in Classical Studies: Aeschylus* (Oxford 2007).
Michelini, A.N., *Tradition and Dramatic Form in the Persians of Aeschylus* (Leiden 1982).
Mitchell-Boyask, R., *Aeschylus: Eumenides* (Duckworth Companions to Greek and Roman Tragedy, London 2009).
Murray, R.D., *The Motif of Io in Aeschylus'* Suppliants (Princeton 1958).
Rosenbloom, D., *Aeschylus: Persians* (Duckworth Companions to Greek

and Roman Tragedy, London 2006).

Rosenmeyer, T.G., *The Art of Aeschylus* (Berkeley, Los Angeles, London 1982).

Sommerstein, A.H., *Aeschylean Tragedy* (Bari 1996).

Thalmann, W.G., *Dramatic Art in Aeschylus's Seven against Thebes* (New Haven and London 1978).

Torrance, I., *Aeschylus: Seven against Thebes* (Duckworth Companions to Greek and Roman Tragedy, London 2007).

Winnington-Ingram, R.P., *Studies in Aeschylus* (Cambridge 1983).

Other scholars mentioned by name in the text

Bollack, J., '*Prometheus Bound*: drama and enactment', in D. Cairns and V. Liapis (eds), *Dionysalexandros: Essays on Aeschylus and his Fellow Tragedians in Honour of Alexander F. Garvie* (Swansea 2006) 79-89.

Brown, A.L., 'Eumenides in Greek tragedy', *Classical Quarterly* 34 (1984) 260-81.

——— 'Prometheus Pyrphoros', *Bulletin of the Institute of Classical Studies* 37 (1990) 50-6.

Griffith, M., *The Authenticity of 'Prometheus Bound'* (Cambridge 1977).

Lawrence, S.E., 'Eteocles' moral awareness in Aeschylus' *Seven*', *Classical World* 100 (2007) 335-53.

McCall, M., 'The secondary choruses in Aeschylus' *Supplices*', *California Studies in Classical Antiquity* 9 (1976) 117-31.

Macleod, C.W., 'Politics and the *Oresteia*', *Journal of Hellenic Studies* 102 (1982) 124-44 (= *Collected Essays* [ed. O. Taplin, Oxford 1983] 20-40).

Scullion, S., *Three Studies in Athenian Dramaturgy* (Stuttgart and Leipzig 1994).

Taplin, O., *The Stagecraft of Aeschylus: the Dramatic Use of Exits and Entrances in Greek Tragedy* (Oxford 1977).

West, M.L., 'The Prometheus trilogy', *Journal of Hellenic Studies* 99 (1979) 130-48.

——— *Studies in Aeschylus* (Stuttgart 1990).

——— 'Ancestral curses', in J. Griffin (ed.), *Sophocles Revisited: Essays Presented to Sir Hugh Lloyd-Jones* (Oxford 1999) 31-45.

White, S., 'Io's world: intimations of theodicy in *Prometheus Bound*', *Journal of Hellenic Studies* 121 (2001) 107-40.

Glossary

anapaests: in this book the term always describes a sequence consisting basically of ∪ ∪ – ∪ ∪ – , neither spoken nor sung, but delivered in a kind of recitative chant, and often (but not exclusively) used by a chorus as it processes into the *orchestra*, or as a prelude to a sung choral ode.

dochmiacs: an excited lyric metre, the commonest forms of which are ∪ ∪ ∪ – ∪ – or ∪ – – ∪ – or – ∪ ∪ – ∪ –.

ekkyklema: a kind of trolley which could be rolled out through the central door of the *skene* carrying a tableau to represent an indoor scene.

epirrhematikon (epirrhematic): a lyric or semi-lyric exchange between a chorus and one or more actors.

hamartia: an error, usually of judgement, but sometimes with a moral connotation.

hybris: behaviour which is calculated to humiliate another person or a god and to assert one's own superiority. It is often misleadingly translated as 'pride' or 'arrogance'. In this book the assumption is that it only secondarily denotes a state of mind rather than an action, and that it does not primarily describe the crossing of a line that separates man from god.

iambics: in this book the term describes the usual metre of spoken dialogue, in which each line consists of x – ∪ – three times (with x representing a syllable which may be either long or short, and with a long syllable often resolved into two shorts).

kommos: a dirge in the form of an *epirrhematikon*.

mechane: a kind of crane which could lift an actor, often playing the part of a god, over the roof of the *skene*. The introduction of the device was probably later than Aeschylus.

orchestra: literally 'the dancing-place' of a chorus, the term is used to describe the whole of the circular (some would say rectangular) space occupied by actors as well as chorus (see *skene*).

parodos: as used in this book the term describes the entrance anapaests (if any) and first song of the chorus.

protagonist: the leading actor of the company of two or three.

satyr-play: a semi-comical burlesque of a mythological theme that was regularly presented by each tragedian after his three tragedies at the Festival of Dionysus. The chorus consisted of mythical satyrs.

skene: the wooden building at the back of the orchestra, in which the actors could change their costumes and their masks. Its central door often represented the entrance to a palace or temple. Whether it had more than one door is disputed. The roof could be used for the appearance of a god or other character. Aeschylus certainly used the *skene* in his *Oresteia*, but many believe that it had not been introduced to the theatre in time for his earlier plays. It is unlikely that in this period there was a raised stage (*skene* in a different sense) which would be the principal area for the actors' performance, as opposed to the *orchestra* of the chorus.

stichomythia: a rapid form of dialogue in which the speakers delivered single (or occasionally double) lines in alternation.

Index